M000247923

USAF PROTOTYPE JET FIGHTERS

◇ PHOTO SCRAPBOOK ◇

Compiled By
TONY R. LANDIS and DENNIS R. JENKINS

specialtypress
PUBLISHERS AND WHOLESALERS

specialtypress
PUBLISHERS AND WHOLESALERS

Specialty Press
39966 Grand Avenue
North Branch, MN 55056
Phone: 651-277-1400 or 800-895-4585
Fax: 651-277-1203
www.specialtypress.com

© 2009 by Tony R. Landis and Dennis R. Jenkins

All rights reserved. No part of this publication may be reproduced or utilized in any form or by any means, electronic or mechanical, including photocopying, recording, or by any information storage and retrieval system, without prior permission from the Author. All text, photographs, and artwork are the property of the Author unless otherwise noted or credited.

The information in this work is true and complete to the best of our knowledge. However, all information is presented without any guarantee on the part of the Author or Publisher, who also disclaim any liability incurred in connection with the use of the information.

All trademarks, trade names, model names and numbers, and other product designations referred to herein are the property of their respective owners and are used solely for identification purposes. This work is a publication of Specialty Press, and has not been licensed, approved, sponsored, or endorsed by any other person or entity.

ISBN 978-1-58007-137-6
Item No. SP137

Library of Congress Cataloging-in-Publication Data

Landis, Tony.
  U.S. Air Force jet fighter prototypes / by Tony R. Landis and Dennis R. Jenkins.
    p. cm.
  ISBN 978-1-58007-137-6
  1. Fighter planes--United States--History--Pictorial works.
2. Research aircraft--United States--History--Pictorial works. 3. Jet planes, Military--United States--History--Pictorial works. I. Title.
  UG1242.F5L38 2008
  623.74'64--dc22
                          2008034473
Printed in China
10 9 8 7 6 5 4 3 2 1

On the Front Cover:
The sixth, and last, General Dynamics YF-16A (74-0750) on a flutter test flight over Edwards, California. Note the ALQ-119 electronics countermeasures (ECM) pod under the wing. The flags on the forward fuselage represent the countries that had ordered the F-16. *(AFFTC History Office Collection)*

On the Back Cover (top):
The first Republic XF-84H (51-17059) at the Air Force Museum prior to being installed in the Research and Development Hangar. The XF-84H was an unsuccessful attempt at using a turboprop engine to achieve the performance of a jet aircraft with better fuel economy. A hideous propeller noise induced headaches and abrupt nausea in the pilots and ground crews and caused the crews to dub the airplane "Thunderscreech." Subliminal ultra-low-frequency sound waves were later identified as the culprit. *(NMUSAF Archives)*

On the Back Cover (bottom):
Two missiles, the Hughes F-98 Falcon and the Boeing F-99 Bomarc, initially received   F-for-Fighter designations. Here, a YF-99 guidance test missile is launched on the Air Force Missile Test Center at Cape Canaveral. Both missiles were soon redesignated, leaving the "F" designation for manned aircraft. *(45th Space Wing History Office)*

On the Title Page:
One of the Lockheed YF-12A Mach 3+ interceptors at Edwards AFB on 30 September 1964. Note the white infrared sensors on the leading edge of each chine. The cut-off chines were significantly different than the   A-12 or SR-71 spy planes. *(National Archives)*

On the Last Page:
The Lockheed Martin X-35C (300) flies over Edwards on 25 January 2001 with Lockheed test pilot Joe Sweeney at the controls. *(Lockheed Martin photo by Judson Brohmer)*

Distributed in the UK and Europe by
Crécy Publishing Ltd
1a Ringway Trading Estate
Shadowmoss Road
Manchester M22 5LH England
Tel: 44 161 499 0024
Fax: 44 161 499 0298
www.crecy.co.uk
enquiries@crecy.co.uk

INTRODUCTION

This seems to happen to us every time we write a book – we find too many interesting photographs! In this case, the larger volume is *Experimental and Prototype U.S. Air Force Jet Fighters* (ISBN 978-1-58007-111-6), published by Specialty Press in early 2008. Since the book covered a multitude of aircraft types, we did not conduct our usual exhaustive search for photos, but nevertheless came away from the various archives with more material than would fit in the 276 pages allocated to us. Therefore, the publisher graciously allowed us another opportunity to do the photo scrapbook that you are reading.

This is not intended to be a definitive work on experimental fighters, but rather a collection of pictures with, hopefully, enough information to be useful to history buffs and modelers.

One note of caution: Many of the photos shown here have color-shifted due to age. As regrettable as this is, there is no easy way to restore the photos to their original condition, but we figured they were well worth publishing.

Like the larger volume, this book spends a few pages covering the fighters made famous during World War II, just as an introduction. A few more pages cover the three unusual designs that resulted from the 1940 Request for Data R-40C competition. Although ultimately powered by relatively conventional piston engines, the Vultee XP-54, Curtiss XP-55, and Northrop XP-56 used innovative aerodynamic configurations in an attempt to radically improve performance; all failed in that goal, and World War II was fought with highly developed, but entirely conventional, fighters such as the Republic P-47 Thunderbolt and North American P-51 Mustang.

The bulk of the pages are devoted to Air Force jet fighters that actually carried an "XF" or "YF" designation (or the predecessor XP/YP monikers). During the 1970s the Air Force did not always apply the designation scheme the way it had been intended, so many aircraft types did not have formal XF or YF models – we covered most of them.

The introduction of the jet engine has, rightfully, been called a revolution. The performance of piston-powered fighters was inching upward at a snail's pace, restricted by the increasing difficulty being encountered in designing more powerful piston engines, as well as the aerodynamic issues of propeller tips that were approaching the speed of sound. Cooling issues, and the drag associated with providing enough air for the radiator or cylinders, was becoming a nightmare. The increasing complexity of the large, heavily turbo-supercharged piston powerplants was taking its toll on reliability and the maintenance crews.

The turbojet engine arrived on the scene producing approximately the same power as the best piston engines then in service. The jet engines had fewer moving parts and were easier and cheaper to produce. Initially, however, they were much less reliable and consumed considerably more fuel. Improved material and better manufacturing techniques radically lowered the failure rates, and advanced designs used substantially less fuel. The introduction of water-alcohol injection and afterburners generated yet more power.

By the time the North American F-100 introduced the Century Series, there seemed to be no limit to performance. The F-100 was the first U.S. fighter capable of exceeding the speed of sound in level flight. Within a few years the Lockheed F-104 became the first Mach 2 fighter. Three different Mach 3 fighters were designed, although only a trio of Lockheed YF-12As actually flew, as it became evident that very high speed was not necessary for most roles.

The last 30 years have seen the development and continual improvement of the augmented turbofan engine, allowing jet fighters to exceed Mach 1 in a vertical climb, often without the use of afterburners. However, the primary focus during this time has been on systems – radar, electronic countermeasures, fire control – and stealth technologies. These are, apparently, more difficult to develop than airframes, resulting in only a handful of fighter designs since the 1970s, instead of the dozens that preceeded them. The resulting development programs have taken a great deal longer.

Consider that the F-100 took an unbelievably short three years from the award of the development contract to the first squadron being declared operational. Contrast that with the Lockheed Martin F-35. The Air Force announced in 2007 that the F-35 systems development phase is scheduled to last more than 12 years, after more than a dozen years of studies and a fly-off. It appears there will not be a need to update this publication in the foreseeable future. Nevertheless, we hope you enjoy it.

Tony R. Landis
Tehachapi, California

Dennis R. Jenkins
Cape Canaveral, Florida

The most famous of the long line of Curtiss fighters was the P-40. By the outbreak of World War II, the P-40 was already obsolete but, nevertheless, it played an important role. This P-40F was used by the NACA to test experimental ailerons. (NASA Langley)

A Boeing P-26A mounted in the 30x60-foot full-scale wind tunnel at the NACA Langley Memorial Aeronautical Laboratory in 1934. Nicknamed Peashooter, this was the first Army fighter to be constructed entirely of metal and to employ a low-wing monoplane configuration. Still, the wings were externally braced and the non-retractable landing gear had streamlined covers. (NASA Langley)

The Seversky P-35 was the first Army single-seat fighter to feature all-metal construction, retractable landing gear, and an enclosed cockpit. The airplane eventually led to the highly successful P-47. The NACA began testing a P-35 in April 1939. (NASA Langley)

The P-39 Airacobra (top) and P-63 Kingcobra were the most successful fighters from Bell Aircraft. Both featured a mid-mounted engine driving the propeller through a long extension shaft under the cockpit. (top: NASA Langley; bottom: NMUSAF Archives)

Lockheed's P-38 Lightning (top) and XP-58 Chain Lightning featured twin booms and tricycle landing gear. The P-38 was probably the Army's best-performing fighter when World War II began. Only a single XP-58 was built. (top: NASA Langley; bottom: Lockheed Martin)

The two most successful Army fighters of World War II were the Republic P-47 Thunderbolt (top) and North American P-51 Mustang. Both aircraft offered outstanding performance and were built in larger numbers than any other U.S. fighters. (NASA Langley)

The Northrop P-61 Black Widow was the first dedicated radar-equipped night fighter developed for the Army and included several concepts later used on the Northrop F-89 Scorpion and later all-weather interceptors. (Gerald H. Balzer Collection)

Perhaps the most unusual idea for a long-range fighter was the North American P-82 Twin Mustang. As the name implies, this was essentially two P-51 fuselages on a common wing. The airplane found limited use in the Korean conflict. (Jim Hawkins Collection)

The first winner of the 1940 Request for Data R-40C competition was the Vultee XP-54. This unusual aircraft was an inverted gull-wing monoplane with twin booms and a single-seat cockpit located in the center section of the magnesium fuselage, just behind a pair of 37mm cannon and two .50-caliber machine guns. (San Diego Air and Space Museum Collection)

The XP-54 was supposed to be powered by a 1,850-hp Pratt & Whitney H-2600 with a two-stage supercharger and counter-rotating propellers. This engine was soon cancelled and replaced by a 2,200-hp Lycoming XH-2470 driving a normal four-blade propeller. Vultee estimated the Lycoming engine would provide a maximum speed of 480 mph at 27,000 feet. (Gerald H. Balzer Collection)

The first XP-54 (41-1210) during taxi tests at the Vultee facility in Downey, California, before its maiden flight. The XH-2470 powerplant never developed its advertised horsepower and encountered numerous development problems, leading to its cancellation in 1943 and effectively sealed the fate of the XP-54. A plan to re-engine the second XP-54 with the 2,350-hp Wright R-2160 Tornado engine driving a set of counter-rotating propellers under the XP-68 designation never materialized. (San Diego Air and Space Museum Collection)

The second XP-54 was largely similar to the first except that it was fitted with armament and a single experimental General Electric XCM turbocharger instead of the earlier Wright TSBB units. The airplane made its maiden flight on 24 May 1944 from Downey to Ontario. Oddly, photographs show the second XP-54 (42-108994) wearing serial number 41-1211. (San Diego Air and Space Museum Collection)

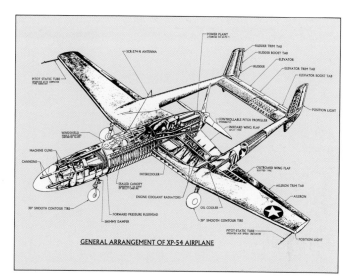

GENERAL ARRANGEMENT OF XP-54 AIRPLANE

The XP-54 was designed around a newly developed NACA "ducted wing" in which airflow was taken in via slots in the leading edge, directed over the engine radiators and intercoolers, and then fed into the engine via ducts in the trailing edge. This was expected to provide a significant reduction in total drag and a corresponding increase in speed, but it did not work out that way. (Gerald H. Balzer Collection)

On 28 October 1943, the first XP-54 was flown to Wright Field for Phase II performance tests. While at Wright Field the airplane carried "Swoose Goose" nose art, a name reportedly coined by Vultee employees in Downey. (Gerald H. Balzer Collection)

The first XP-54 undergoing maintenance before its maiden flight. The top of the engine was easily accessible from the large wing, but access to other areas of the fuselage required maintenance stands due to the height above the ground. (Gerald H. Balzer Collection)

The second place entry in the R-40C competition was the Curtiss XP-55, a radical "tail first" design with a single pilot sitting ahead of the engine and pusher propeller. To gain confidence in the basic configuration, Curtiss built a CW24-B "flying mockup" powered by a single 275-hp Menasco C68-5 engine driving a two-blade propeller. (Gerald H. Balzer Collection)

The first XP-55 (42-78845) was rolled out of the Curtiss-Wright plant in St. Louis on 26 June 1943, draped in tarpaulins for security. The airplane was towed to an isolated part of the ramp for engine run-up tests. By 7 July 1943, the airplane had been disassembled and moved via truck to Scott Field, Illinois, where Harvey Gray made its maiden flight on 13 July 1943. (Gerald H. Balzer Collection)

Throughout the development of the XP-55, Curtiss-Wright designers explored other applications of the basic design since they believed that the swept wing and nose-mounted, free-floating elevator would be adaptable to many missions, including high-speed reconnaissance, heavy bombardment, and cargo transports. This Model P-274 four-engine transport featured a double-deck fuselage to carry troops and cargo. Although wind-tunnel models (left) were tested in March 1943, no actual hardware was built. (Gerald H. Balzer Collection)

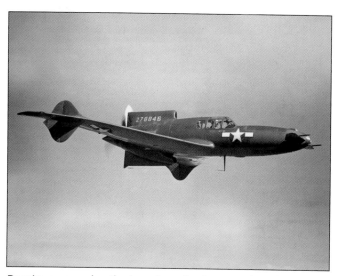

The second XP-55 (42-78846) was essentially identical to the first, being too far along in manufacture to incorporate the lessons learned from the crash of the initial airplane. Note the graceful curvature of the wing-mounted vertical surfaces, typical of many designs from the 1930s and 1940s. The single Allison V-1710-95 used a 10-foot-diameter Curtiss propeller. (Gerald H. Balzer Collection)

Despite a general enthusiasm from Curtiss test pilots, Army pilots were greatly concerned about the stall characteristics of the XP-55. These were never completely sorted out, and directly resulted in the loss of two of the three prototypes. A jet-powered version, called the CW24-C, was briefly considered by Curtiss but never embraced by the Army. (Gerald H. Balzer Collection)

The early days of flight tests involved tents and radios, not elaborate control rooms. Talking on the radio is project manager C. W. Scott, with John Stratton in the center, and an unknown person in the white cap. (Lawrence D. Lee Collection via Gerald H. Balzer)

Arguably one of the great names in aviation manufacturing, Curtiss-Wright, would disappear as an airframe company soon after World War II ended. Note the Curtiss-Wright St. Louis emblem on the airplane in the foreground. (Gerald H. Balzer Collection)

The last R-40C winner was the Northrop XP-56. This is the first XP-56 (41-786) under construction at the Northrop facility in Hawthorne, California, with the wing and fuselage not yet mated. The single Pratt & Whitney R-2800 radial engine will be installed in the open compartment in the fuselage. The original short, vertical stabilizer is shown here. (Gerald H. Balzer Collection)

The cockpit of the XP-56 was a tight fit. On the left were the controls for the throttle, supercharger, propeller, and landing gear. On the right were the parking brake and radio controls. The standard flight instrumentation was on the front panel. (Gerald H. Balzer Collection)

The armament for the XP-56 consisted of four .50-caliber machine guns (shown) and a pair of 20mm cannon. The machine guns were completely contained within the nose, but the cannon used the compartment under the pilot for ammunition. (Gerald H. Balzer Collection)

The remains of the first XP-56 after an accident on 8 October 1943. Northrop test pilot John Myers suffered minor injuries. Considering that the airplane tumbled backward across the desert two times, the basic structure was relatively intact. (Gerald H. Balzer Collection)

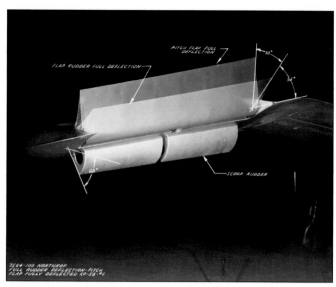

The rudder control on the first XP-56 followed the basic design used on the Northrop N-9M research airplanes. The drag rudder consisted of a combination of a spoiler-type surface rotating out of the lower wing surface and a compensating upward deflection of a pitch trim surface on the upper wing. (Gerald H. Balzer Collection)

The initial engine runs on the first XP-56 were conducted at Hawthorne in March 1943. These tests uncovered some issues with the gearbox mounting, and Northrop modified the installation to reduce vibration. After initial taxi tests at Hawthorne, the airplane was trucked to Muroc on 10 May. (Gerald H. Balzer Collection)

The second XP-56 (42-38353) was equipped from the beginning with the enlarged dorsal stabilizer that had been added to the first airplane. To improve rudder action, the control linkage was disconnected from the air brakes that provided rudder control and connected to air valves located in wingtip ducts. When the rudder pedal was deflected, the valves moved to prevent air from flowing through the duct in the appropriate wingtip and directed it to a bellows that opened the corresponding air brake, causing the airplane to turn. (Gerald H. Balzer Collection)

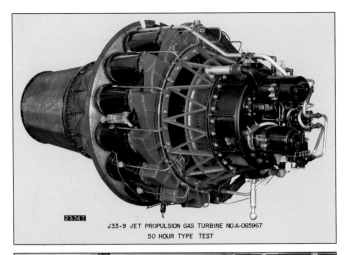

23747

J33-9 JET PROPULSION GAS TURBINE NO.A-065967
50 HOUR TYPE TEST

A General Electric I-16 (J31) on a test stand at Wright Field in August 1945. This engine generated 1,610-lbf of thrust from a package the same size and weight as the original 1,250-lbf I-A, which had been little more than a license-produced version of Frank Whittle's W.1X engine. (NMUSAF Archives)

The 4,000-lbf General Electric I-40 (J33) was the ultimate development of the Whittle design in the United States. It was 103 inches long, 51 inches in diameter, and weighed 1,775 pounds. The engine powered the Lockheed P-80, among others. (NMUSAF Archives)

The Pratt & Whitney J48 was a license-produced version of the Rolls-Royce RB.44 Tay and powered the North American YF-93, Lockheed F-94, and the Navy's Grumman F9F Panther. Over 4,000 J48s were produced between 1949 and 1959. (NMUSAF Archives)

Two Bell Aircraft products fly in formation, a P-63A (42-69417) Kingcobra and a P-59A (44-22609) Airacomet. Initial plans to introduce the P-59A into operational service were squashed by its relatively poor performance, and only 50 were ultimately produced. (National Archives)

A P-59A was tested in the full-scale wind tunnel at the NACA Langley Memorial Aeronautical Laboratory at Hampton, Virginia. The square wingtips are an easy way to identify this as a later aircraft instead of one of the XP-59A prototypes. (National Archives)

On 5 January 1945, the first rescue mission conducted by a Bell helicopter took place when Jack Woolams bailed out of a P-59A near Lockport, New York. Floyd Carlson and Dr. Thomas C. Marriott flew a Bell Model 30 and, guided by Joe Masham flying another P-59A, rescued the unfortunate Woolams. (AFFTC History Office Collection)

The P-59A was a completely conventional design, although it used a large, laminar-flow wing optimized for high-altitude operation since that is where the Army and Bell expected the airplane to operate. The aircraft was fitted with an engine mounted on either side of the fuselage under the wing roots. (AFFTC History Office Collection)

Bell test pilot Jack Woolams in the cockpit of an Airacomet, with Walt Polanski (without hat) and Joe Brown (with hat) looking on. Woolams became chief test pilot for Bell in 1944, and was the first pilot to fly the X-1 research airplane. (AFFTC History Office Collection)

A few Airacomets were modified as drone directors with a second cockpit installed forward of the main cockpit. The front cockpit was open (no canopy) on most of the modified aircraft, although a few had small bubble canopies installed. (AFFTC History Office Collection)

The thirteen YP-59As were powered by 1,610-lbf General Electric I-16 (J31) turbojets, which were essentially license-built Whittle W.2s. The engines were hung in fairings below the fuselage, making access easy, if somewhat awkward for the maintenance crews. This was fortunate, given their frequent need for servicing. (Tony Landis Collection)

The round wingtips were only used on the three XP-59A experimental models before they were replaced by square units that were easier to produce. Forward visibility from the cockpit was good, although the wing and air inlet interfered with downward vision. (NMUSAF Archives)

The "ground control team" and their equipment at Muroc during a P-59A test flight. It is difficult to compare this to the modern control centers used by the F-22 and F-35 fighters during their flight-tests at Edwards AFB. (AFFTC History Office Collection)

All three XP-59As and some of the YP-59As carried a yellow "Bell Aircraft Corp" script on the nose, along with national insignia on the wings and fuselage. Unlike modern aircraft, there was a distinct lack of caution and warning stenciling. (AFFTC History Office Collection)

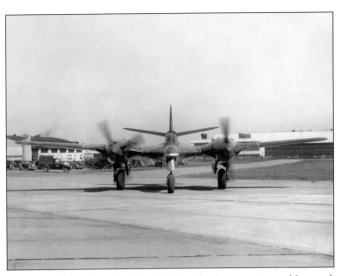

The extreme streamlining on the McDonnell XP-67 (42-11677) predated by several decades the blended wing-body concept used by modern aircraft such as the Lockheed F-16. Unfortunately, the additional wetted area (the total surface area on the outside of the airplane) created excessive frictional drag and actually decreased performance. The XP-67 used a pair of Continental XI-1430-1 engines with General Electric D-2 turbochargers in nacelles on the wings driving conventional tractor propellers, although the nacelles look like they should contain rear-mounted jet engines. In fact, McDonnell proposed installing an Allison V-1710 or Rolls-Royce/Packard V-1650 engine with two-stage supercharger in the forward portion of the nacelle and a (stillborn) 2,000-lbf General Electric I-20 (XJ39) jet engine in the rear portion, replacing the turbocharger. The loss of the only airplane eliminated any further consideration of this idea. (National Archives)

The XP-67 (42-11677) was the first aircraft designed and built by the McDonnell Aircraft Company and showed the innovative thinking that would allow the company to dominate the fighter market during much of the postwar era. (NMUSAF Archives)

On 1 February 1944, during the fourth test flight at Scott Field, Illinois, the engines were unintentionally overspeeded, burning out the bearings and resulting in an emergency landing. The airplane was returned to St. Louis for repairs. (National Archives)

During its brief flight-test career, the first XP-67 accumulated 43 flight hours. With the exception of the first four flights at Scott Field, all of the flights were at Lambert Field. The second airplane ordered as part of the original contract was never completed. (National Archives)

A fire on 6 September 1944 ended the flying career of the XP-67. Initially, the fire was contained to the right engine nacelle, but after landing, the wind blew the flames across the fuselage, causing considerable damage. (National Archives via Kim McCutcheon)

All of the XP-67 flights used conventional, four-blade propellers. There were, however, proposals to modify the XP-67 with counter-rotating propellers in an attempt to improve performance. These were initially delayed by the lack of availability of the new propellers, then by a loss of interest on the part of the Army because of the disappointing flight-test results. Like the jet-powered concepts, these never came to pass, although at least some of the basic engineering was accomplished. (National Archives)

The Northrop XP-79B (43-52437) under construction. Contrary to many published reports, the XP-79B was never intended to ram enemy aircraft. This myth seemingly began with a misinterpretation of the armored leading edges intended to protect the hypergolic propellant tanks on the rocket-powered XP-79. Note the openings for the .50-caliber machine guns above the nose landing gear. (Gerald H. Balzer Collection)

Unlike the stillborn, rocket-powered XP-79s, the XP-79B was powered by a pair of Westinghouse 19B (XJ30) axial-flow turbojet engines. Note the unusual landing gear that used four struts, two retracting into each engine nacelle. (National Archives)

The Westinghouse XJ30 was an axial-flow turbojet, unlike the centrifugal-flow engines built at the time by General Electric and Allison. This resulted in a much smaller diameter, allowing it to fit into the small nacelles on the XP-79B. (Gerald H. Balzer Collection)

Northrop test pilot Harry Crosby took the XP-79B on its only flight on 12 September 1945. The airplane initially appeared stable, but 14 minutes after takeoff it went into an unintentional roll after Crosby made several steep banks to the right and left. The XP-79B continued to roll until its wings were vertical, then plunged to the ground from an altitude of 7,000 feet. Crosby managed to bail out of the airplane, but was apparently struck by the wing before opening his parachute; the rip cord had not been pulled when his body was recovered. (Gerald H. Balzer Collection)

The pilot flew from a prone position that, in theory, allowed him to endure up to 12-g positive accelerations. (Gerald H. Balzer Collection)

The XP-79B used ducted air intakes on the wingtips for lateral control, much like the second XP-56. (Gerald H. Balzer Collection)

The thirteen Lockheed YP-80As were generally similar to the earlier XP-80A, but, in contrast with the initial prototypes, were manufactured within the mainstream Lockheed organization instead of by Skunk Works. Here, the first YP-80A (44-83023) has had its rudder replaced (or repainted), eliminating the last two digits of its serial number. This airplane made its 45-minute maiden flight on 13 September 1944 and was flown the following day to the NACA Ames Aeronautical Laboratory at Moffett Field, California, for high-speed diving tests. (NMUSAF Archives)

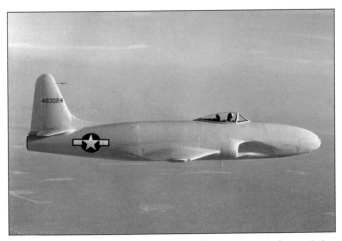

The performance of the P-80 was significantly better than existing piston-engine types, and the Army wanted a photo-reconnaissance aircraft with similar characteristics. On 1 July 1944, a contract change order converted the second YP-80A (44-83024) into the XF-14 reconnaissance configuration. The six 0.50-caliber machine guns in the nose were replaced by a set of cameras shooting through a window in the lower fuselage section in front of the nosewheel. This differed from later RF-80 reconnaissance models, which had cameras on the side of the nose ahead of the air intakes. (NMUSAF Archives)

The forward fuselage for the XP-80 (44-83020) under construction at Skunk Works in Burbank, California. Note the space for the intake duct, sweeping upward from its entrance below the canopy to a position midway up the fuselage where it could feed the engine face. (Terry Panopalis Collection)

The single XP-80B (44-85200) was modified into the P-80R (usually, incorrectly, called the XP-80R) to set a world's speed record on 19 June 1947, flown by Col. Albert Boyd. The aircraft ended its career as a trainer at Sheppard AFB and is now displayed at the National Museum of the United States Air Force. (NMUSAF Archives)

These are early production P-80As, not prototypes, but the photograph is significant in that it shows concurrent production of P-38 Lightnings in the background. The P-80 was much faster than the P-38 but suffered from a relatively short combat radius. (Lockheed Martin)

In November 1944, the original XP-80 (44-83020) was retired from its testing duties and transferred to the 412th Fighter Group to continue exploring jet aircraft tactics before finishing its career as a testbed for the Goblin engine. The photo at left shows the airplane in storage at Muroc AAF prior to being delivered to the Museum Storage Depot at Orchard Park, Illinois, on 8 November 1946. The aircraft was subsequently transferred to the Smithsonian in 1949. The photo at right shows the restored XP-80 prior to being displayed at the National Air and Space Museum in Washington, D.C. (left: Jim Hawkins Collection; right: Terry Panopalis Collection)

Above: *The Convair XP-81 was a large fighter, but was very clean aerodynamically. The bubble canopy was located ahead of the wing and afforded the pilot good vision in just about all directions, although the turbojet air intakes obscured some of the over-the-shoulder view. Air for the turboprop engine came from an inlet around the propeller spinner.* (National Archives)

Left: *Initial flights in the first XP-81 (44-91000) were made using a Packard-built V-1650 Merlin piston engine since the TG-100 (XT31) turboprop was not ready. The radiator for the Merlin was in a fairing just behind the nose gear, with an oil cooler and carburetor air intake in the nose just under the propeller spinner. The entire installation was borrowed from a P-51.* (National Archives)

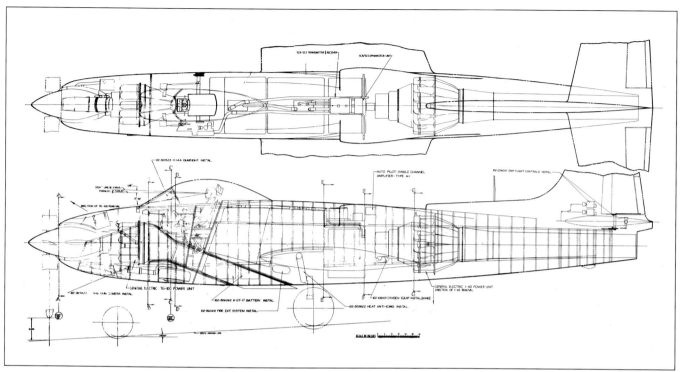

This inboard profile of the XP-81 shows the 2,300-shp General Electric TG-100 (XT31) turboprop installed in the nose, while the 4,000-lbf General Electric I-40 (J33) turbojet was mounted amidships and exhausted through a long tailpipe, much like the contemporary Republic F-84 and North American F-86. Unfortunately, neither engine delivered its advertised power output. (National Archives)

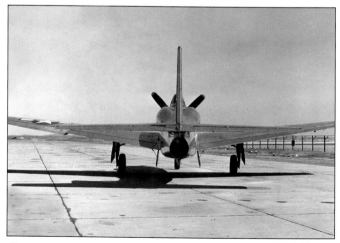

The two turboprop XP-81s only logged 69 flights totaling about 42 hours. Because TG-100 delivered only 1,400 shaft horsepower (shp), the performance of the turboprop-powered XP-81 was no better than that of the Merlin-powered version. (National Archives)

Air for the I-40 turbojet was drawn from a pair of intakes mounted on the fuselage shoulder behind the cockpit canopy. The air had a very short run to the engine face, unlike other fighters that used nose inlets for their engines. (National Archives)

The Bell XP-83 was dynamically stable longitudinally, but it exhibited a slight pitching tendency due to fuel slosh. Much like the earlier P-59A, there was a marked tendency for the XP-83 to oscillate laterally (snake) just after take-off and in rough air, and a slight tendency to hunt directionally. While considered adequate for normal flying, the handling was judged inadequate "for acrobatics or spin recovery." Wind-tunnel tests showed that an 18-inch extension of the vertical stabilizer would cure most of the stability problems. (Lloyd Jones Collection via Bill Norton)

The first XP-83 (44-84990) at the Bell facility in Niagara Falls, New York, on 2 August 1945. The airplane was heavier than expected since Bell had used existing parts (such as landing gear struts) to reduce costs and meet the schedule. (AFFTC History Office Collection)

The first XP-83 in late 1945. At this point it was in storage at Wright Field and was rolled out for various air shows and other displays. The following year it was made flight worthy and used for airborne ramjet experiments. (NMUSAF Archives)

This walk-around of the first XP-83 shows the general resemblance to the P-59A design. The Phase II performance tests took place between 27 July and 31 August 1945 at the Bell facility in Niagara Falls, New York. The performance of the XP-83 was disappointing, and no series production was ordered. Apart from its range, the airplane offered no significant advantages over the Lockheed P-80 that was already in production. Both XP-83s were subsequently used as testbeds for various projets, with the first XP-83 being destroyed in a crash on 4 September 1946, and the second prototype was scrapped in early 1947. (National Records Center, St. Louis Collection)

The second Republic YF-84F (51-1345) and YRF-84F (51-1828) show the differences between the two airplanes. Externally, the wing-root intakes were similar since most of the changes were to the internal ducting, but the noses of the two aircraft were very different. (National Archives)

The first XP-84 (45-59475) at the Republic facility in Farmingdale, New York, before it was rolled out. The airframe was very streamlined, and probably represented the ultimate straight-wing configuration. (National Records Center, St. Louis Collection)

The first YF-84J (51-1708) takes off for its maiden flight on 7 May 1954 with Republic test pilot Russell M. "Rusty" Roth at the controls. Note that the nose gear is mostly retracted and the main gear are beginning to retract. (AFFTC History Office Collection)

The first XF-84H (51-17059) at Farmingdale. The XF-84H used a 5,850-shp Allison XT40 turboprop that also provided 830 lbf. The engine was mounted in the normal location and drove the propeller through extension shafts under the cockpit. (Cradle of Aviation Museum)

"Republic Two, Air Force Zero"

Republic Aviation developed the novel XF-91 Thunderceptor (top) with wings that were wider and thicker at the tips than at the wing root. It also had a hybrid rocket jet/rocket propulsion system. The propeller tips of the turboprop-powered XF-84H "Thunderscreech" were supersonic, producing unbearable noise levels for both ground crew and pilot. The two prototypes were flown only twelve times. Neither type entered service with the U.S. Air Force.

Hank Caruso aerocatures are well known in the aviation industry, and this one shows two of Republic's more bizarre attempts to advance the state of the art of fighter design using the basic F-84 concept. (©2005 by Hank Caruso, reproduced by permission)

The second XF-84H (51-17060) landing at Edwards. Note the deployed ram air turbine (RAT) just ahead of the vertical stabilizer. A hideous propeller noise caused ground crews to dub the aircraft "Thunderscreech." (NMUSAF Archives)

The second XP-85 (46-524) was the first to fly and was used for most of the flight-test program. In these 15 July 1948 photos, the airplane is being loaded into a Boeing B-29B (44-84111) named Monstro for a captive carry flight to evaluate the effect of carrying the parasite. The first free flight did not take place until 28 August 1948. Note the emergency landing skid protruding forward of the inlet. (National Archives)

The XP-85 mockup was displayed next to a B-36A at the St. Louis Air Show on 17 October 1948. Ironically, on the same day, the second prototype was forced to make an emergency landing at Muroc, when the pilot encountered severe turbulence and loss of directional stability while trying to recover to the B-29. (National Archives)

The second XP-85 on its ground transportation trailer and without the emergency landing skid that proved to be so useful during the flight-test program. This shows the diminutive size of the 15-foot-long Goblin, which was the smallest jet fighter ever built for the U.S. Air Force. (Francis Allen Collection)

The wooden XP-85 mockup under construction at the McDonnell facility in St. Louis, Missouri. This mockup was equipped with folding wings, and was frequently mated to a wooden mockup of a B-36 bomb bay. (Francis Allen Collection)

One of the XF-85s late in its career after it was equipped with vertical surfaces on the wingtips. These had been suggested by NACA test pilot Scott Crossfield, but did little to restore directional stability during the approach to the B-29. (Francis Allen Collection)

The first North American XP-86 (45-59597) during an early test flight. During its early development, the XP-86 was hurriedly redesigned with a swept wing, and flight tests quickly showed that the straight-wing fighter was obsolete. Note the buzz numbers on the aft fuselage and lower wing surface, typical of the late 1940s and early 1950s. (National Records Center, St. Louis Collection)

During the Cold War, some truly bizarre concepts were evaluated. Here, North American proposed an unmanned version of the F-86 that could be launched from a Convair B-36. The "F-86 Missile" would carry a nuclear warhead to a target 3,000 miles from its launch point, allowing the B-36 to stay safely out of Soviet airspace. At the time of launch, the B-36 would have flown over 3,000 miles, taking almost 17 hours. (National Records Center, St. Louis Collection)

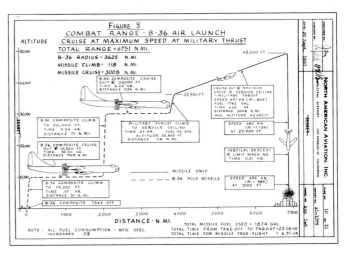

Because the swept wing was not thoroughly understood, wind-tunnel testing on the XP-86 was even more important than usual, and large-scale models like this spent a great deal of time in both NACA and university facilities. (National Records Center, St. Louis Collection)

The initial production batch of F-86As used flush-fitting electrically operated gun-muzzle doors that maintained a smooth outer mold line. These muzzle doors opened automatically when the guns were fired. (Air Force Historical Research Agency Collection)

This was the gun installation in the XP-86 mockup. The gun bay door could serve as a step for the pilot, although the door had to be closed by the ground crew since there was no method of doing so from the cockpit. (National Records Center, St. Louis Collection)

The F-86A .50-caliber machine gun installation. The retractable flush-fitting muzzle doors were made of frangible metal that would shatter if the guns inadvertently fired while the doors were closed. (Air Force Historical Research Agency Collection)

The third XP-86 (45-59599) was very similar to production F-86As. Here the airplane is on a test flight carrying 2.75-inch FFAR rockets, along with a bevy of cameras under the wings to record the rockets' behavior. (AFFTC History Office Collection)

Not a prototype, per se, but an interesting experiment. This F-86F at the NACA Ames Aeronautical Laboratory has been modified with a boundary-layer control system. The pumps and other equipment were mounted in the large bulge under the fuselage. (National Archives)

The second XP-86 (45-59598) with North American test pilot George S. "Wheaties" Welch in the cockpit. Remarkably, on 7 December 1941, Welch had shot down four Japanese aircraft over Pearl Harbor while flying a Curtiss P-40. (National Archives)

The XP-86 flight-test program was not without its problems. This is the second airplane (45-59598) after its twelfth flight, on 25 March 1948, when its right main landing gear collapsed while landing at Muroc. (National Records Center, St. Louis Collection)

The fifth production F-86A (47-609, later NACA 135) was tested in the 40x80-foot full-scale wind tunnel at the NACA Ames Aeronautical Laboratory. Here it is being lowered into the test section. Note the lack of an engine. (National Archives)

North American built two TF-86F two-seat trainers. The first one crashed in 1954, killing North American test pilot Joe Lynch. The second TF-86F (53-1228) served as a chase plane at Edwards for many years. (AFFTC History Office Collection)

The YF-86D (50-577) was transferred to Ames as NACA 149. The NACA flew the airplane between 26 June 1952 and 15 February 1960. One experiment added vortex generators to improve longitudinal and lateral control. (National Archives)

The first YF-86H (52-1975) introduced the 8,920-lbf General Electric J73 turbojet. To accommodate the new engine, the fuselage was stretched two feet, increased in diameter, and used a larger air intake. (AFFTC History Office Collection)

The first McDonnell XF-88 (46-525) shortly after it was rolled out of the McDonnell plant in St. Louis, Missouri. McDonnell pilots made 41 flights before turning the airplane over to the Air Force for the Phase II performance tests at Edwards beginning on 15 March 1949. The results were disappointing, confirming the need for afterburning engines. (National Records Center, St. Louis Collection)

Another photo of the first XF-88 after its rollout. In August 1950, this airplane was modified into the XF-88B propeller research vehicle. The XF-88B spent most of its time at the NACA Langley Aeronautical Laboratory. Following the completion of their testing, both XF-88s sat in a junkyard at the nearby Langley AFB for several years and were eventually scrapped. (Stan Piet Collection)

It is uncertain if the XF-88 ever fired rockets in the air, but the second prototype (46-526) did on the ground on 25 April 1950. The airplane was suspended under a crane and there was a person in the cockpit. (AFFTC History Office Collection)

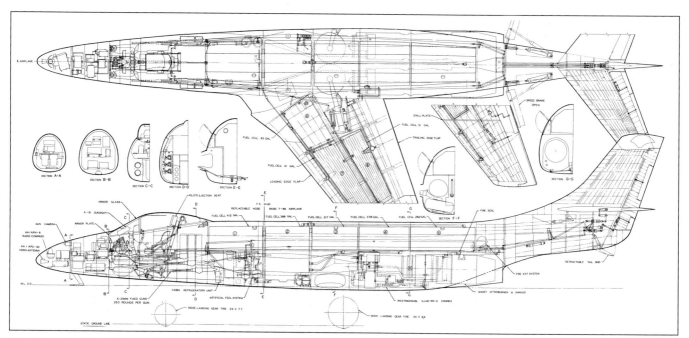

The inboard profile of the production F-88A shows the location of the six 20mm cannon and their ammunition, and also shows the tail skid on the extreme aft fuselage. Because of funding constraints, no F-88As were ever manufactured. (National Records Center, St. Louis Collection)

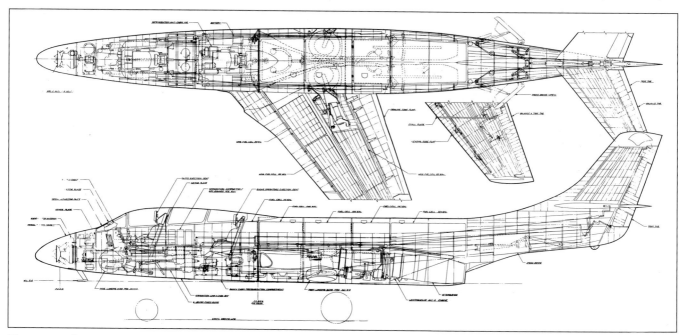

The proposed two-seat F-88 deleted the 412-gallon fuel cell directly behind the pilot and added a second seat under a longer canopy. The six 20mm cannon were retained and performance (except for range) was expected to be similar. (National Records Center, St. Louis Collection)

The gloss-black paint used on the Northrop XF-89 (46-678) might have made the airplane look sinister, but it was undoubtedly uncomfortable for the crews in the high desert at the Muroc test base. What few markings the XF-89 carried were painted in red, except for the full-color national insignia. The large bullet in front of the horizontal stabilizer – used only on the XF-89 – stands out in this photo. Northrop test pilot Fred C. Bretcher took the XF-89 on its maiden flight on 16 August 1948. (Northrop via Tony Chong)

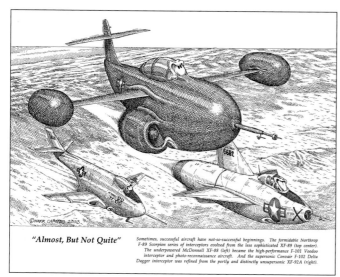

"Almost, But Not Quite"   Sometimes, successful aircraft have not-so-successful beginnings. The formidable Northrop F-89 Scorpion series of interceptors evolved from the less sophisticated XF-89 (top center). The underpowered McDonnell XF-88 (left) became the high-performance F-101 Voodoo interceptor and photo-reconnaissance aircraft. And the supersonic Convair F-102 Delta Dagger interceptor was refined from the portly and distinctly unsupersonic XF-92A (right).

In "Almost, But Not Quite," Hank Caruso captures three early proto-type airplanes that eventually morphed into successful designs. The evolution of the F-89 was the most straightforward, with production aircraft being generally similar to the experimental XF-89 except in the sort of details you would expect to evolve during a test program. (©2003 by Hank Caruso, reproduced by permission)

During Project Gun-Val in October 1954, a single F-89C (51-5795) was equipped with a pair of T-110E3 rocket launchers on the nose. The T-110 used Armour Research Foundation T-131 spin-stabilized 2.75-inch (70 mm) rockets fed from a magazine in the nose. Each launcher carried 25 rounds and had a rate of fire of 27 rounds per minute. (National Archives)

As a result of a 1948 evaluation of the XF-87, XF-89, and Navy Douglas XF3D-1, on 4 January 1949 the Air Force ordered 48 production F-89As and directed Northrop to complete the second XF-89 (46-679) as the YF-89A service test aircraft. In March 1949, the name Scorpion was approved, the suggestion originating with the crews at Edwards who thought the upward-curving rear fuselage and high tail looked a lot like the creature with the deadly stinger in its tail. The YF-89A is shown here on 30 August 1950. (AFFTC History Office Collection)

The first Lockheed XF-90 (46-687) with the wingtip fuel tanks that were frequently carried during the flight-test program. Lockheed test pilot Tony LeVier took the XF-90 on its maiden flight from Muroc on 3 June 1949. (Terry Panopalis Collection)

The first XF-90 being towed from its hangar at Muroc. Initially, the first airplane was powered by non-afterburning Westinghouse J34s, and was significantly underpowered. Afterburners helped, but the XF-90 was still too heavy for the available power. (National Archives)

The cockpit of the first XF-90 shows the typical 1950s flight instrumentation. About the only electronic systems were the radios and radio-navigation devices. Production aircraft would have included a small gun-laying radar. (AFFTC History Office Collection)

Both XF-90s fly in formation, with the first airplane at the top. The two prototypes were essentially identical after the first XF-90 received its afterburning engines. (Lockheed Martin)

The XF-90s included provisions for six 20mm cannon, three below each air intake. The shell ejection chutes may be seen just inboard of the leading edge of the wing. (Lockheed Martin)

The first XF-90 in Burbank prior to its first flight. After the test program, this aircraft was sent to the NACA Lewis Flight Propulsion Laboratory in Cleveland for use as a structural test article, and its fate is unknown. The second aircraft was used as a ground-test specimen during the Operation TUMBLER/SNAPPER nuclear test in Nevada during April 1952. The hulk has recently been decontaminated and sent to the Air Force Museum, where it will eventually be featured in a diorama depicting the atomic testing. (Lockheed Martin)

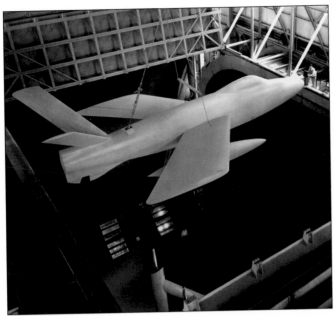

A full-scale model of the original Republic XF-91 design in the NACA Ames Aeronautical Laboratory 40x80-foot wind tunnel. The V-tail was supposed to reduce drag, but wind-tunnel testing was inconclusive and the configuration resulted in some structural issues. It was dropped from the design in May 1947. (National Archives)

The second XF-91 (46-681) being loaded with liquid oxygen and alcohol propellents for its Reaction Motors XLR11 rocket engine. This was the same basic engine that had powered the Bell X-1 series and Douglas D558-2 Skyrockets. The engine made the XF-91 the first supersonic "operational type" aircraft. (Cradle of Aviation Museum)

The first XF-91 (46-680) on 23 January 1950 at Edwards. As completed, both prototypes used conventional empennages. Late in the test program, the second XF-91 would receive a modified version of the originally proposed V-tail. (AFFTC History Office Collection)

The first prototype shows the unusual landing gear arrangement. The dual-wheel main gear retracted outward into the thick wingtips that were a major characteristic of the design. The conventional nosewheel retracted forward. (Cradle of Aviation Museum)

The two prototypes pose together near the end of the program. By this time, the first (left) had a radar nose and revised air intake, while the second had a V-tail. Each is carrying small external fuel tanks. The YRF-84F may be seen in the background. (National Archives)

Unusually, the Air Force Museum made a mistake when it repainted the first XF-91 for display. The restoration staff marked the airplane as the second prototype (46-681) instead of the first (46-680). It took several years to correct the error. (NMUSAF Archives)

The cockpit of the second XF-91, showing the toggle switches used to ignite the four chambers of the XLR11 rocket engine along the top of the panel. The switch to turn the turbopump on is located at the extreme left. (Cradle of Aviation Museum)

The cockpit mockup for the proposed production F-91A. The rocket engine controls have been moved to a quadrant near the jet throttle on the left console. Note the large scope for the Hughes MX-1179 fire-control system. (Cradle of Aviation Museum)

The Convair XF-92A (46-682) on the seaplane ramp at the Convair facility in San Diego, California. The XF-92A was an aerodynamic demonstrator intended to prove the delta-wing concept for the XP-92 ducted-rocket-powered interceptor. As it turned out, the XP-92 was cancelled before the XF-92A made its first flight on 18 September 1948, but the Air Force was sufficiently intrigued by the delta-wing concept that it allowed the demonstrator to continue, much to the benefit of the future F-102 program. (San Diego Air & Space Museum via Robert E. Bradley)

After its flight-test program, the XF-92A was used as a traveling display by the Air Force Recruiting Service. For unknown reasons, it was then sent to the Franklin County Airport in Sewanee, Tennessee, sometime in 1965. The airplane sat there with a steel ladder on the side of the fuselage for four years, allowing vandals an opportunity to break into the cockpit and steal the instruments. Eventually, the ladder was removed and the canopy bolted shut. Then vandals started shooting at the windshield and fuselage. The Air Force Museum recovered the airplane in 1969, and it is currently on display in the Research & Development Hangar. (Courtesy of Bill Kershner)

The XF-92A was painted in this unusual camouflage to play "MiG 23" in the movie Jet Pilot, but in the end was not used in the film. The colors were black-green and sky blue with red lettering and a white outline. (AFFTC History Office Collection)

An accident on 14 October 1953 ended the flying career of the XF-92A. While Scott Crossfield was landing on the lakebed, the nose-wheel collapsed. Since the Convair F-102 was scheduled to fly later that month, the XF-92A was permanently grounded. (NASA Dryden)

The first North American YF-93A (48-317) showing the unusual "YF" buzz numbers favored by the company for its prototype fighters. The original flush, NACA-style air inlets are obvious even from this angle. (National Records Center, St. Louis Collection)

The first prototype with the final inlet design that was added late in its career. Although the NACA-style inlets achieved their goal of minimizing drag, they did not provide sufficient airflow to the engine, resulting in a significant power loss. (National Archives)

The YF-93A showed an obvious lineage to the F-86 it had evolved from (it had originally been designated F-86C), especially in the empennage and canopy. The dual-wheel main landing gear is noteworthy. (Boeing Historical Archives)

The YF-93A was the last of the three penetration fighter competitors to take to the air when North American test pilot "Wheaties" Welch made the maiden flight on 25 January 1950. The McDonnell XF-88 won the competition. (Boeing Historical Archives)

USAF Prototype Jet Fighters

In June 1951, both YF-93As were turned over to the NACA Ames Aeronautical Laboratory for tests of the flush air intakes. After a series of experiments, the NACA eventually fitted both prototypes with conventional air intakes that proved more efficient. The airplanes were used by the NACA as flight-test and chase aircraft well into the mid 1950s, and played an important role in testing components for most of the Century Series fighters. Both aircraft were retired and scrapped in the late 1950s. (Boeing Historical Archives)

The Lockheed-funded interceptor demonstrator (civil registration N94C) made its maiden flight on 19 January 1950, with Tony LeVier at the controls. The Air Force was sufficiently impressed that in February 1950 it purchased the airplane as the YF-97 and assigned it a military serial number (50-955); it was subsequently redesignated YF-94C. Here the airplane shows the original F-94A-style forward fuselage, and that the small wing root extension fillet found on all other P-80 variants was deleted from the new F-94C wing. The F-94C also used a swept-empennage to eliminate a high-frequency vibration at high Mach numbers. Officially, the C-model was the only variant named Starfire, although as the years have passed, all F-94s seem to have inherited the name. (National Archives)

The eleventh F-94C (50-966) was used by Lockheed for a variety of publicity and test purposes and was painted in special Starfire livery for much of its early career. The new nose on the F-94C housed a Hughes E-5 fire-control system and four groups of six 2.75-inch folding-fin aerial rockets (FFAR). Over the course of its production and service life, the F-94C was progressively upgraded with improved ejection seats, variable-position dive brakes, and a better drag chute. Beginning with the 100th F-94C, a pod containing 12 FFARs was mounted on each wing leading edge, doubling the armament. (National Archives)

Not all "F" designations were assigned to manned aircraft. In 1951, an "unmanned fighter" and an "unmanned interceptor" were issued designations within the traditional fighter series since it was expected their functions would eventually supplement, if not supplant, manned aircraft. This decision was quickly reversed in August 1955, and no missiles entered operational service with an F designation.

In 1947, the Army awarded Ryan Aeronautical a development contract for the AAM-A-1 Firebird missile as project MX-799, the first truly viable air-to-air missile project. The first launch took place in October 1947. This North American F-82B (44-65179) is carrying four development missiles on 18 April 1949. (National Archives)

In 1947, the AAM-A-2 (Air-to-Air Missile – Army) designation was assigned to a Hughes missile developed as project MX-798, which was later named Falcon. The first experimental missiles were ground launched in 1948 in a long-lived investigation of aerodynamic configurations. This missile is from 20 April 1949. (National Archives)

Initially, the Falcon was being developed as a "bomber defense" missile, intended to be launched by U.S. bombers against Soviet interceptors. Most of these concepts were tube launched from the rear of the bomber since it was expected most attacks would come from that direction. Test missiles were launched from the ground and from a B-25. This configuration is from 7 July 1949. (National Archives)

In 1950, the Army dropped the idea of a bomber defense missile, although it was briefly revived during the WS-110A (B-70) competition. Therefore, the Falcon was redirected as an anti-bomber missile to be launched by interceptors, and the development was moved to project MX-904. At the same time, the missile was designated XF-98. This configuration is from 26 October 1950. (National Archives)

By the time this photo was taken, the F-98 designation was ancient history, and the interim GAR-1/2/3/11 designations had given way to the final AIM (Air Intercept Missile) nomenclature. From the left are the nuclear-armed AIM-26A (it still says GAR-11 in the data block), the infrared (IR) guided AIM-4C, the semi-active radar homing (SARH) AIM-4A, the IR-guided AIM-4G, and the SARH-guided AIM-4H. (National Archives)

The second missile to receive an F-for-Fighter designation was the Boeing Bomarc. Two different types of test missiles were manufactured. Experimental XF-99 propulsion test vehicles were used to evaluate the liquid-fueled booster that would accelerate the interceptor to ram-jet ignition speed. The YF-99 designation was reserved for missiles that included prototype guidance systems, but in August 1955, before any YF-99s could be built, the Air Force discontinued the use of aircraft-type designators for missiles, and Bomarc was redesignated IM-99 (for Intercept Missile). This is a 1956 launch from Cape Canaveral, Florida. (45th Space Wing History Office)

An XF-99 propulsion test vehicle on its transport trailer at Cape Canaveral on 30 June 1953. (45th Space Wing History Office)

This YIM-99A guidance test missile looks like the production articles that would later stood alert. (45th Space Wing History Office)

The Martin B-57s that had been used during development at Patrick AFB were later used to check the ability of the Eglin AFB test range to accommodate Bomarc operational testing on Santa Rosa Island. Bob Ferry and Tom Sorber were the crew on this 12 November 1959 flight. (National Archives)

The Bomarc launch site on Santa Rosa Island near Eglin AFB. In the background are two research-and-development shelters, and the prototype operational shelter is on the right. This picture is easily mistaken for a winter scene because the sand on Santa Rosa Island is so white and fine it looks like snow. (National Archives)

Several aircraft were used to test the Bomarc guidance system, including this Lockheed NF-94B (51-5502) and Martin JB-57B (52-1497), shown at Patrick AFB, Florida. At least one other B-57B (52-1493) also participated in the tests. (National Archives)

The North American F-100 was the first of a new breed that was capable of supersonic speeds in level flight. The F-100 would lend its designation to the "Century Series" of fighters that defined American airpower during the early part of the Cold War. Between May 1953 and December 1956, seven different operational fighter designs – the F-100, McDonnell F-101, Convair F-102, Lockheed F-104, Republic F-105, and Convair F-106 – made their first flights, expanding the speed envelope well past Mach 2. In this family portrait, clockwise from top left are an F-100, F-101A, F-102A, F-104A, YF-105A, and F-106A. (AFFTC History Office Collection)

USAF Prototype Jet Fighters

An F-100 wind-tunnel model undergoing testing at the NASA Ames Research Center. This is an early F-100 configuration, judging by the lack of landing flaps on the inboard wing trailing edge. The small canards on the nose of the model are noteworthy. (NASA Ames)

The first YF-100 (52-5754) flies over the North Base facility at Edwards late in its test career. Note that the buzz number on the nose has now been replaced with a "YF-100" marking. (AFFTC History Office Collection)

The first YF-100 sits on the North American Aviation ramp prior to being shipped to Edwards for flight testing. Note the missing instrumentation boom below the intake and the original "FW" buzz number on the nose. (Boeing Historical Archives)

There were no XF-101s or YF-101s, so the test program was conducted using the initial production aircraft. This is the third production F-101A (53-2420) landing at Lambert Field in St. Louis after a test flight. Note the Voodoo markings on the nose. (National Archives)

The first F-101A (53-2418) during final assembly at the McDonnell plant in St. Louis, Missouri. Originally conceived as a long-range escort for the Strategic Air Command, the F-101 went on to become a nuclear-armed fighter-bomber for the Tactical Air Command. Note the Voodoo markings on the vertical stabilizer and that the 20mm cannon ports. (Terry Panopalis Collection)

The first two F-101As (53-2418 and 53-2419) fly over Edwards in 1956. Note the buzz numbers on the bottom of the fuselage, a location that would also be used by the early F-4 Phantom IIs. The first F-101A is now on display at the Pueblo Weisbrod Aviation Museum in Pueblo, Colorado. (AFFTC History Office Collection)

After completing its test program, the first F-101A was bailed to General Electric to test the J79-GE-1 turbojet. Here is the aircraft on a test flight over Edwards on 28 September 1958. The aircraft was subsequently retired to Amarillo AFB in Texas as a ground maintenance trainer. (AFFTC History Office Collection)

The first F-101A on the lakebed at Edwards. The airplane had been rolled out of the factory in August 1954 and, after completing ground trials in St. Louis, it was shipped to Edwards. McDonnell test pilot Robert C. Little took the F-101A on its maiden flight on 29 September 1954, reaching Mach 0.9 at 35,000 feet. Note the faired-over 20mm cannon ports. (Terry Panopalis Collection)

The fourth Convair YF-102 (53-1780) poses with the ninth production F-102A (53-1799). The differences between the two aircraft are easily noticed in this view. The production models were 11 feet longer and used an Area Rule or "coke-bottle" shape that included fairings on each side of the aft fuselage. (Terry Panopalis Collection)

The third F-106A (56-453) and a late-model F-102 (56-1317) show the differences between the two interceptors. Originally conceived as the follow-on to the F-102 known as the F-102B, the F-106 evolved into a completely new aircraft that shared little other than the basic configuration. (AFFTC History Office Collection)

Not a prototype, but unusual. This F-102A (57-0835) was loaned to the Federal Aviation Administration for use on the SST program from April to December 1970. The aircraft carried civil registration N300 and an FAA logo on the side of the intake. (AFFTC Museum Collection)

A staged photo on the Edwards lakebed showing the fifth YF-102 (53-1781) during pre-flight operations. The non–Area Rule fuselage shows up well in this view. (National Archives)

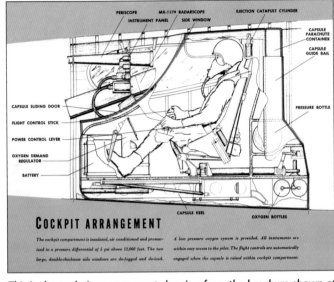

COCKPIT ARRANGEMENT

The cockpit compartment is insulated, air conditioned and pressurized to a pressure differential of 5 psi above 12,000 feet. The two large, double-thickness side windows are de-fogged and de-iced.

A low pressure oxygen system is provided. All instruments are within easy access to the pilot. The flight controls are automatically engaged when the capsule is raised within cockpit compartment.

The Republic XF-103 was, in theory, a competitor of the Convair F-102. Everybody realized, however, that Alexander Kartveli's Mach 3 design was too futuristic to be produced anytime soon, and the program was carried mostly as a technology demonstration effort. This is the cover of a brochure. (Cradle of Aviation Museum)

This is the cockpit arrangement drawing from the brochure shown at left. This arrangement is for the XF-103 that used a flush canopy, and shows the location of the ejection capsule, periscope, and MX-1179 radarscope. Another version of the airplane used a more conventional canopy but was generally similar. (Cradle of Aviation Museum)

The proposed XF-103 escape capsule after the first drop test from a Boeing JB-47 at Edwards in 1957. While the capsule survived the drop without any major damage, the slightly-too-small parachute was ripped to shreds from the air loads. (National Archives)

An XF-103 wind-tunnel model undergoing testing at the NASA Ames Research Center. This is a somewhat confusing configuration since it shows an early-style raised canopy with the late-model large-diameter fuselage, air intake, and ventral stabilizer. (NASA Ames)

Close-up of the extended Falcon missiles on the full-scale XF-103 mockup. As originally envisioned, the fire-control system and Falcon missiles would have been identical to those installed on the Convair F-102, and the speed and altitude estimates for the XF-103 drove the design of those items. (National Records Center, St. Louis Collection)

Along with the full-scale mockup with a flush canopy, Republic also built a second full-scale mockup of the forward fuselage with a raised canopy (foreground). Kartveli wanted a conventional canopy on his interceptor, but the Air Force insisted on the flush design that is usually shown. (National Records Center, St. Louis Collection)

Manufacture of the first prototype had been underway prior to program cancellation. This is the first production escape capsule under construction at the Republic plant in Farmingdale, New York. Note the heavy-gage construction required to withstand the airloads of a Mach 3+ ejection. (Cradle of Aviation Museum)

Due to the tight security surrounding the XF-103 program, few photos exist of the first prototype under construction, such as this horizontal stabilizer that had been completed by the time the program was terminated. In the end, all of the XF-103 parts were scrapped, along with much of the documentation. (Cradle of Aviation Museum)

The original full-scale mockup for the Lockheed XF-104 was hand-crafted entirely of wood. The two experimental aircraft were faithful to this mockup, including the use of air intakes without the center shock cones on production aircraft. The less sohpisticated inlets worked well with the interim J65 engines. (Lockheed Martin)

With the full-scale XF-104 mockup in the background, workers are busy assembling various parts of the YF-104As on 15 March 1954. Noteworthy is the sign in the back of the shop that reads "First Flight March 1st, 1954 9:00 am, Subject to Weather Only." Skunk Works missed that date by a mere three days. (Lockheed Martin)

The first XF-104 (53-7786) on the lakebed preparing for a flight with its F-94C (50-957) chase plane behind it. (Dave Menard Collection)

The official maiden flight of the first XF-104 (53-7786) was made from the lakebed at Edwards on 4 March 1954 with Lockheed test pilot Tony LeVier at the controls. Unfortunately, the landing gear would not retract, and LeVier landed 20 minutes later. (Lockheed Martin)

A good view of the smaller tail assembly used on the first XF-104. This photo was taken during pre-first-flight operations at Edwards on 28 February 1954. Note the unusual position of the national insignia and the Northrop XF-89 in the background. (Lockheed Martin)

This front view of the first XF-104 on the ramp at Edwards on 22 June 1956 is a good example of why the Starfighter earned the description "missile with a man in it." The two XF-104s were shorter than later models and were equipped with Curtiss-Wright J65 engines and the distinctive air intakes without the half-cones used by production models. When powered by the non-afterburning J65-W-6 turbojet, the XF-104 could not exceed Mach 1 in level flight, but could in a shallow dive. (AFFTC History Office Collection)

The second YF-104A (55-2956) was used for the official rollout ceremony on 16 April 1956. For security reasons, the intakes had been covered with metal fairings, as the half-cones were still classified at the time. It would be another six months before the air intakes would be revealed to the public. Note the faired-over port for the newly developed General Electric T-171 (M61) 20mm rotary cannon. (Lockheed Martin)

The first XF-104 (53-7786) and first YF-104A (55-2955) pose together on the ramp at Edwards. The larger size and revised air intakes on the YF-104A are noticeable in this view. The XF-104s, YF-104s, and early-production examples all used downward-firing ejection seats that would be replaced in later examples after the loss of some crewmembers at low altitudes. (Terry Panopalis Collection)

USAF Prototype Jet Fighters

Hundreds of hours were spent in various wind tunnels developing the XF-104 and later F-104 configurations. Smaller models like this one were generally used for high-speed tests, while larger models were used in the low-speed wind tunnels. (Lockheed Martin)

The pilot and ground crew pose with the first XF-104 at Edwards after completing its 500th flight on 28 December 1956. The XF-104 flight-test program eventually spanned three years before this aircraft was retired. (Lockheed Martin)

Preflight operations on the first XF-104 (53-7786) and one of the YF-104A prototypes at Edwards. The two XF-104s proved to be the first in a long line of Starfighters that eventually numbered in excess of 2,500 aircraft, mostly for international air forces. At the time, this represented Lockheed's most successful post–World War II aircraft production program. (Lockheed Martin)

This was the first Republic F-105B (54-0104) that did not carry a "YF" or "JF" designation, but was nevertheless dedicated to the flight-test program for its entire career. As shown on this 16 April 1959 flight, it lacked any flight-test markings, but carried a long air data probe on the nose. Note the bomb on the outer wing pylon, along with three external fuel tanks. (National Archives)

The third YF-105B (54-0102), parked on the ramp at Edwards, shows the glazed panel behind the canopy that was only used on the two YF-105As and four YF-105Bs. (National Archives)

The last dedicated test aircraft was this F-105B (54-0111), shown on 21 November 1958 in the skies over Eglin AFB. Note the Thunderchief markings on the vertical stabilizer. (National Archives)

USAF Prototype Jet Fighters

The YF-105A demonstrated it could perform as a "buddy tanker" using a special centerline store equipped with a drogue refueling hose. This capability was incorporated into most F-105Bs but was never used and later deactivated. Here a Lockheed F-104A (56-0761) prepares to take on fuel from the second YF-105A (54-0099) during a demonstration flight over Edwards. (Mike Machat Collection)

The third YF-105B being rolled out of the Republic factory at Farmingdale, New York. Production F-105Bs were generally similar to the YF-105Bs except for the glazed panel behind the canopy and the continual evolution of the fire-control system. The F-105 was the largest single-seat fighter yet built for the U.S. Air Force, but was also among the fastest aircraft in the inventory. (Cradle of Aviation Museum)

"The Final Thrust of the Sabre"

The North American Aviation F-107 was based on the airframe and wings of the F-100 Super Sabre. It's trademark dorsal air intake and sharply tapered nose gave the design a streamlined, rakish appearance. Unfortunately, sexy looks were not the deciding factor in the competition between the F-107 and the Republic F-105. When it lost the competition, the F-107 became the last fighter aircraft to bear the North American Aviation name.

© Hank Caruso, ASAA 2004

North American test pilot Robert Baker prepares to take the first F-107A (55-5118) on its initial taxi run on 6 September 1956. Note the large "F-107A" marking that was located just aft of the cockpit on the first aircraft only; the other two aircraft used smaller markings on the radome. (National Archives)

"The Final Thrust of the Sabre" aerocature shows the first F-107A "Ultra Sabre." Contrary to most reports, and the aerocature, there was not a true competition between the F-105 and F-107; the North American airplane was developed strictly as insurance in case Republic failed. (©2004 by Hank Caruso, reproduced by permission)

The first F-107A comes in for a safe landing at the conclusion of its second flight on 1 October 1956 with its 16-foot drag chute billowing behind. This was in contrast to the harrowing first flight the month before when the chute failed to deploy and the aircraft ran off the runway and onto the lakebed, causing the nose landing gear to fail. (National Archives)

The engineless second F-107A (55-5119) on the North American Aviation ramp. Note the small "F-107A" marking under the windscreen. The F-107 development was paid for out of production funding, and therefore the aircraft were not considered "YF" prototypes. (National Archives)

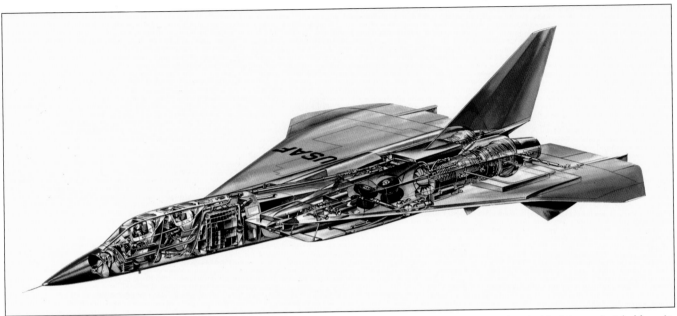

This cutaway gives a good look inside the planned North American F-108. The electronics compartment just behind the cockpit held equipment for the ASG-18 radar and navigation systems. The three GAR-9 missiles were on a rotary launcher in the center of the airplane, followed by the main landing gear that had a complicated landing gear folding sequence to fit into the fuselage. The thrust reversers on the drawing do not match the engineering description, and it's hard to see how they would have worked as drawn. (Scott Lowther Collection)

Over the course of the F-108 program, North American built several full-scale mockups, including this one of the forward fuselage showing the internal structure of the nose radome compartment, although the ASG-18 antenna is not shown. (National Archives)

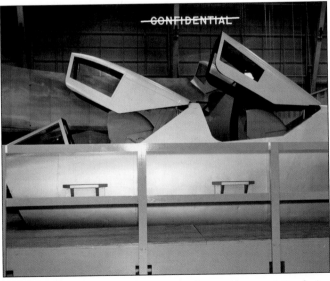

Another full-scale mockup showing the front and rear canopy design for the F-108. As the design evolved, the rear canopy window was reduced in size and eventually ended up as a small circular porthole instead of a real window. (National Archives)

Even the General Electric J93 engine had its own full-scale mockup. This view shows the original clamshell thrust reverser that would later be deleted in favor of a simpler flat-plate design that rotated over the nozzle from the top and bottom. (National Archives)

Work on the F-108 full-scale mockup was a continual work in progress. This view shows it at an interim stage in which the mock-up had been given a coat of gloss-white paint but still retains the rectangular aft cockpit windows. (National Archives)

Close-up of the ASG-18 and GAR-9 displays in the aft cockpit of the F-108 mockup. The UHF radio controls and page printer are just to the left of the displays. The back seater did not have any flight controls and had very limited visibility. Compare these cockpit photos with those on page 85 that show the Lockheed YF-12A that ultimately used the ASG-18 and GAR-9. (Boeing Historical Archives)

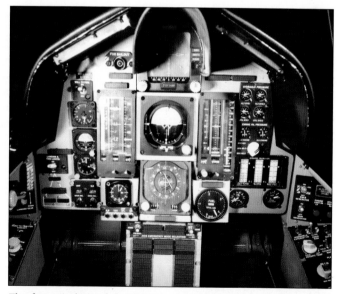

The front cockpit of the F-108 was a mixture of traditional round dials and the vertical tape instruments that found favor during the early 1960s. Note the large WILL TO FIRE switch at the upper left that allowed the weapons systems officer to fire (both crewmembers had to concur since the GAR-9s were nuclear armed). (Boeing Historical Archives)

Although the designation XF-109 was never officially assigned to any aircraft, it has been commonly applied to the Bell D188A. This was a private venture for a Mach 2+ VTOL fighter powered by eight General Electric J85 turbojets. Two engines were mounted horizontally in the rear fuselage and fed by cheek-type air intakes mounted on the sides of the rear fuselage. Two other J85s were mounted vertically in the fuselage behind the cockpit to provide lift during vertical takeoff and landing, but they were shut down for ordinary horizontal flight. The other four engines were mounted in two pairs in moveable pods at the wingtips. (Terry Panopalis Collection)

Bell built this full-scale mockup of the D188A to show potential customers, but ultimately none were found. (Scott Lowther Collection)

A Bell Aerosystems artist concept of the D188A operating from a remote location. (Scott Lowther Collection)

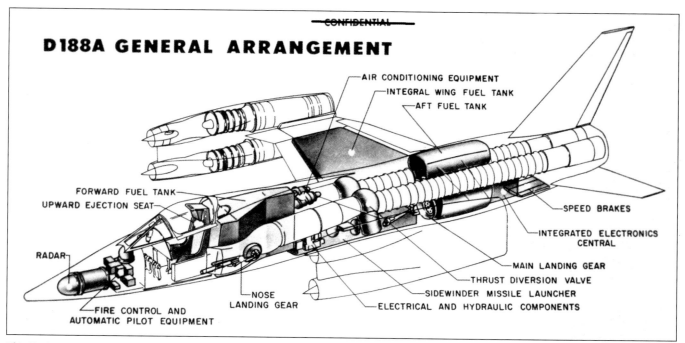

CONFIDENTIAL

D188A GENERAL ARRANGEMENT

AIR CONDITIONING EQUIPMENT
INTEGRAL WING FUEL TANK
AFT FUEL TANK

FORWARD FUEL TANK
UPWARD EJECTION SEAT

SPEED BRAKES

INTEGRATED ELECTRONICS CENTRAL

RADAR

MAIN LANDING GEAR
THRUST DIVERSION VALVE
SIDEWINDER MISSILE LAUNCHER
ELECTRICAL AND HYDRAULIC COMPONENTS

FIRE CONTROL AND AUTOMATIC PILOT EQUIPMENT

NOSE LANDING GEAR

This D188A general-arrangement drawing shows the location of most of the major internal systems, but differs from the mockup since it shows "thrust diverter valves" amidships instead of vertically mounted J85 engines; it also lacks the intakes on the aft fuselage shown on the mockup. It is likely that Bell continually evaluated the propulsion system in an attempt to simplify it. (Scott Lowther Collection)

The Air Force and Navy provided approximately $17 million in Phase I funds for the program, resulting in a full-scale mockup, 600,000 engineering manhours, and 3,500 wind-tunnel hours. At some point, it appears a dedicated mockup of the Navy variant was also built. Nevertheless, the United States did not fund further development of the D188A, and no official designation was ever assigned. The general concept was later taken up by West Germany in the E.W.R-Sud VJ-101C. (Jay Miller Collection)

The first McDonnell F-110A (BuNo 149405/62-12168) at Langley AFB on 2 January 1962 as it was originally delivered to the Air Force for evaluation. After this evaluation, the Department of Defense announced that the F-110A would become the standard Air Force tactical fighter, and on 30 March 1962 issued a contract for a single F-110A (62-12199) and two RF-110A reconnaissance variants (62-12200/201). Since the F-110A was a derivative of a Navy aircraft, there were no XF-110A or YF-110A aircraft. Note that "Phantom II" has been added below the F-110A marking, bringing into question the exact timing of the name change from Spectre versus the designation change to F-4C. (National Archives)

This is the F3H-G/H mockup that led to the F4H (F-4) series. The basic shape of the future Phantom II is readily identifiable despite the single-seat cockpit and the unbent wingtips and horizontal stabilizer. (National Archives)

The sharper nose profile of the first production F-4A (BuNo 143388) shows up well in this view and gives a good evolutionary comparison between the F3H mockup at left and the first F-110A above. (National Archives)

The first two F-110A aircraft (149405/62-12168 and 149406/62-12169) fly formation over the snow-covered landscape near St. Louis, Missouri. At this point the aircraft were still carrying their Navy bureau numbers instead of the soon-to-be-assigned Air Force serial numbers, as well as the large Tactical Air Command badges on the tail that were a short-lived standard. Note the location of the buzz numbers under the aft fuselage, and the semi-recessed mounting for the four AIM-7 Sparrow III air-to-air missiles. (National Archives)

High over the Nevada landscape, the first two F-110As (149405/62-12168 and 149406/62-12169) fly formation during a mission out of Nellis AFB in 1962. Note that the "F-110A" markings have been removed from the nose, although the TAC badges remain. (National Archives)

The first YRF-4C (62-12200) became the first YF-4E, which was later modified with a fly-by-wire control system and finally ended its flight-test career with canards added to the top of the intakes as part of the control configured vehicle (CCV) program. (National Archives)

The third production F-4C (63-7409) on the ramp at Edwards. This aircraft would later be designated as an NF-4C and would have a long flight-test career, finally being retired to the Arizona boneyard in April 1991. (Terry Panopalis Collection)

The third YF-4E prototype was converted from an F-4D (65-0713) and was much closer to the production configuration than the hastily converted YRF-4C had been. The aircraft was later used to test a rudder constructed from boron composite. (NMUSAF Archives)

The first YF-4E (62-12200) is shown at the McDonnell Douglas plant in St. Louis after receiving the fly-by-wire modification and a white, blue, and dark-blue paint scheme. This aircraft is now on display at the National Museum of the United States Air Force. (NMUSAF Archives)

The second F-110A (149406/62-12169) on the ramp at Nellis AFB in March 1962. The two F-110As were essentially Navy F-4Bs, although at some point they were equipped with Air Force standard radios and beacons to allow them to be integrated into the Air Force range structure. Note the "thin" wing that did not have the bump added later for the wider wheels and tires used on all subsequent Air Force Phantoms, and that the "F-110A" markings have already been removed from the nose. (National Archives)

There were no XF-111 or YF-111 aircraft. This is the unpainted second F-111A (63-9767) after a test flight at Edwards in May 1965. Initially, this aircraft was the testbed for the Mark 1 navigation and attack system. In 1966, the aircraft was bailed to Pratt & Whitney to solve the continual inlet-engine compatibility issues that plagued the F-111 and TF30 engine and was instrumental in the redesign of the translating cowls (Triple Plow I) and blow-in doors (Triple Plow II). It is now on display at the Octave Chanute Aerospace Museum in Illinois. (Terry Panopalis Collection)

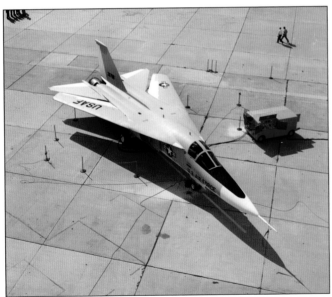

The first F-111A prototype (63-9767) during its rollout ceremony at the General Dynamics facility in Fort Worth, Texas, on 15 October 1964. During the ceremony, the wings were swept using power from the attached ground cart. This aircraft made its 22-minute maiden flight on 21 December 1964, and the first full wing-sweep transition from 16 to 72.5 degrees was made during the second flight on 6 January 1965. This aircraft is currently on display at the Air Force Flight Test Center Museum at Edwards. (National Archives)

USAF Prototype Jet Fighters

The fourth F-111A (63-9769) was used primarily as the spin test aircraft. Here it is shown being towed from a hangar in December 1965, carrying four dummy Hughes AIM-54 Phoenix missiles that would be used by the Navy F-111B variant. (National Archives)

The second F-111A (63-9767) in flight with its wings swept back to the full 72.5 degrees. This aircraft spent most of its early flight-test career unpainted. Despite a variety of initial problems, and a bad reputation with the press and Congress, the F-111 went on to a relatively successful career. (AFFTC History Office Collection)

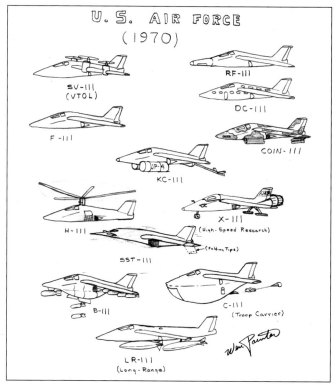

During the late 1960s and early 1970s, variants of the F-111 were proposed to fill a variety of missions as part of Secretary of Defense Robert S. McNamara's "commonality" concept. Unofficially titled "McNamara's Air Force," this artwork by Wen Painter shows every conceivable variation on the F-111. (Artwork by Wen Painter)

The first (59-4987) and third (59-4989) Northrop N-156Fs (F-5A) take off for a test mission out of Edwards. Note that the first aircraft says "Air Force" instead of "U.S. Air Force" on its forward fuselage. There were no XF-5A or YF-5A aircraft, although it is common practice to call the three original N-156F airplanes YF-5As, and some sources indicate the third airplane was delivered as a YF-5A. (NMUSAF Archives)

The clean lines of the third N-156F (59-4989) show up well in this view, and it looks every bit the single-seat T-38 that it was. This aircraft made over 400 test flights and was finally retired to the National Museum of the United States Air Force in 1970. (NMUSAF Archives)

The third F-5A (59-4989) prototype with the first two production F-5A aircraft (63-8367 and 63-8368). The first two production aircraft joined the test fleet in 1963. The first overseas order for F-5As was from Norway, which ordered 64 aircraft plus 4 attrition replacements on 28 February 1964. Eventually, 1,197 F-5A/B/C/D aircraft were manufactured. (NMUSAF Collection)

Northrop Grumman's modified F-5E Shaped Sonic Boom Demonstrator (SSBD) aircraft over Edwards in August 2003. The Defense Advanced Research Projects Agency (DARPA) and NASA investigated a method of shaping the sonic boom generated by a supersonic aircraft to reduce the overpressure to acceptable levels for flight over populated areas. All SSBD flights were flown from the Northrop facility at Plant 42 in Palmdale and went over Harper Dry Lake, where an array of pressure sensors has been assembled to monitor sonic boom overpressures. Baseline data had already been collected from conventional supersonic fighters. (NASA photo by Carla Thomas)

The first N-156F (59-4987) carrying external wing fuel tanks, Sidewinder missiles on the wingtips, and a weapon on the centerline store position. Note the Northrop logo on the vertical stabilizer and the odd buzz number on the fuselage. (NMUSAF Archives)

The first N-156F (59-4987) in flight over Edwards. The first flight took place on 30 July 1959, and Northrop test pilot Lew Nelson exceeded Mach 1 in a shallow dive without the use of afterburners. (AFFTC History Office Collection)

USAF Prototype Jet Fighters

The Lockheed YF-12A was the Air Force's last-ditch attempt to find a Mach 3 interceptor after the earlier cancellations of the Republic XF-103 and North American F-108 programs. The YF-12As were modified versions of the CIA A-12 reconnaissance aircraft, but carried the Hughes ASG-18 radar and GAR-9 missiles originally developed for the F-108. After the YF-12A program was cancelled, the aircraft were allocated to a joint NASA–Air Force test program. NASA pilots flew chase missions in F-104s from December 1969 through February 1970 prior to taking over flying duties themselves. Shown here is F-104N (NASA 811) flying chase on the second YF-12A (60-6935). (AFFTC History Office Collection)

The second YF-12A (60-6935) in the livery that was first shown to the public – overall natural metal with black chines and wing leading edges and only cursory Air Force markings. Later the aircraft would receive their overall black paint scheme. (Lockheed Martin)

Above: *Full-scale forward fuselage mockup of the proposed F-12B production version. Originally known internally as the AF-12, the Air Force assigned the official YF-12A designation early in the test program.* (Lockheed Martin)

Left: *The first YF-12A (60-6934) under construction at the original Lockheed Skunk Works facility in Burbank, California. Clearly visible is the Hughes AN/ASG-18 pulse-Doppler radar that was the most powerful unit of its kind at the time of its debut.* (Lockheed Martin)

Flight crew about to board a YF-12A for an attempt at the absolute speed record at Edwards. On 1 May 1965 the first and third YF-12As were used to set several Fédération Aéronautique Internationale (FAI) Class C-1 Group 3 (turbojet-powered landplanes) absolute records, including a sustained altitude of 80,257.65 feet (Col. Robert Stephens and Lt. Col. Daniel Andre) and a speed over a 15/25-km closed course of 2,070.101 mph (Col. Robert Stephens and Lt. Col. Daniel Andre). (National Archives)

The Hughes ASG-18 fire-control system mounted in the nose of a YF-12A. This unit had been developed for the cancelled North American F-108 Rapier, although some thought had been given to using it in an advanced version of the Convair F-106. The radar used a 40-inch dish antenna, allowing it to detect B-47-size targets at ranges approaching 100 miles. The basic technology from the system was later used to develop the AWG-9 used in the Grumman F-14 Tomcat. (AFFTC History Office Collection)

NASA ground crews busy at work on the second YF-12A (60-6935) during a rare rainy day at Edwards. The vapor is from purging the liquid oxygen system. (Mick Roth)

A proposed paint scheme for the YF-12A during the NASA flight-test program. It would have been interesting to see the Mach 3+ aircraft wearing this colorful livery. (NASA Dryden)

A model of the YF-12A is prepared for a run in the 10x10-foot transonic wind tunnel at the NASA Lewis Research Center in Cleveland, Ohio. This model reflects the later configuration where the infrared sensors have been removed from the chine. (National Archives)

The second YF-12A (60-6935) during a test mission out of Edwards on 11 December 1969. Note the Air Force Systems Command (AFSC) shield and outstanding unit ribbon carried on the vertical stabilizer. (AFFTC History Officer Collection)

The first YF-12A (60-6964) was trucked to Groom Lake in July 1963, and made its maiden flight on 7 August with Lockheed test pilot Jim Eastham at the controls. As this photo of the airplane landing after that flight shows, the fuselage chines were originally not painted black (although the wing leading edge was). The raised cockpits used on the YF-12A were different from the reconnaissance models, as were the forward radome and chine. The infrared sensors have not yet been added to the leading edge of the chines. (Lockheed Martin)

The third (60-6936), in the foreground, and first (60-6934) YF-12As are prepared for early morning test flights at Edwards. (Lockheed Martin)

The aft cockpit of the YF-12A contained all the controls for the radar and missile system as well as the large scope for the Hughes ASG-18 radar and navigation maps. Compare this installation to the F-108 back cockpit shown on page 69. (Lockheed Martin)

Pilot's control panel of the YF-12A. Note the strip-type instruments used for speed and altitude information. The YF-12A was the only member of the Blackbird family to use this type of instrumentation that had also been proposed for the F-108. (Lockheed Martin)

There were no XF-15 or YF-15 aircraft. This is the first F-15A (71-0280) during its maiden flight on 27 July 1972 with McDonnell test pilot Irving W. Burrows at the controls. Bright orange markings had been added between the rollout and the first flight. (AFFTC History Office Collection)

The first F-15A rolled out under its own power at the McDonnell Douglas plant in St. Louis on 26 June 1972. After the ceremony, the aircraft was disassembled, loaded aboard a Lockheed C-5A Galaxy, and transported to Edwards. (National Archives)

The fourth F-15A (71-0284) was one of the first displayed to the public, at a 1973 event at Edwards. Like most early F-15s, the airplane was air superiority blue with orange visibility markings. Note the black stripes on the inside of the vertical stabilizer. (Dennis R. Jenkins)

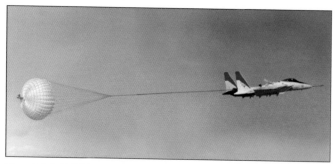

The eighth F-15A (71-0287) was the dedicated spin test prototype, shown here during a spin chute test. Fortunately, the recovery parachute was never needed during the test program. This was the only F-15 prototype originally painted white, which was done to aid in photography during spin recovery operations. The aircraft was later used by the NASA Dryden Flight Research Center in the HIDEC (Highly Integrated Digital Electronic Control) program to develop a computer-assisted engine-control system that lets a plane land safely with only engine power if its normal control surfaces are disabled. The aircraft has been retired. (NMUSAF Archives)

McDonnell Douglas and the Air Force modified an unneeded Category II test F-15A (72-0119) into the "Streak Eagle" in an effort to set new time-to-climb records. The eight record-setting flights took place in January and February of 1975 at Grand Forks AFB in North Dakota. As an example, Streak Eagle climbed to 65,620 feet (20,000 meters) in 122.94 seconds (just over 2 minutes). The airplane eventually went to 98,430 feet (30,000 meters) in 207.80 seconds (3.46 minutes). (U.S. Air Force photo by SSgt. Herman J. Kokojan)

The prototype General Dynamics YF-16 (72-1567) poses with the first YF-16A (75-0745) at the latter's rollout ceremony at the General Dynamics facility in Ft. Worth, Texas, on 21 October 1976. The sharper nose profile of the YF-16 is clearly visible in this view. (National Archives)

The first YF-16 (72-1567) under construction at General Dynamics in Fort Worth. Like most prototypes, the airplane was essentially hand-made. The F-16 is one of the last American fighters made primarily from aluminum alloy. (General Dynamics)

General Dynamics proposed this variant of the F-16 with forward-swept wings for the DARPA-funded Forward Swept Wing (FSW) demonstrator program. DARPA ultimately selected Grumman to build the X-29. (General Dynamics)

The second YF-16 (72-1568) pulls up behind a tanker during a test mission in 1974. As delivered, the aircraft wore an innovative "broken sky" camouflage that combined a light blue (similar to the Air Superiority Blue worn by the early F-15s) with patches of white that were supposed to resemble clouds. The paint scheme was not deemed effective and was soon replaced by an overall light gray. (National Archives)

Photo Scrapbook

As a prelude to the AFTI F-16 program, the first YF-16 (72-1567) was modified with intake-mounted canard surfaces during the controlled-configured vehicle (CCV) tests. The YF-16 CCV made its first flight in the spring of 1976 but was damaged in a landing mishap on 24 June. Repairs took about six months, and the aircraft was returned to flight status in early 1977. (General Dynamics)

With the intake canards removed, the YF-16 CCV was relegated to testing other advanced systems. Here is the aircraft on 10 June 1976 carrying two AIM-7 Sparrow and two AIM-9 Sidewinder missiles. The last flight of this aircraft took place on 31 June 1977. It is currently hanging in the Virginia Air and Space Center in Hampton, Virginia. (AFFTC History Office Collection)

A derivative of the YF-16 CCV, the AFTI (Advanced Fighter Technology Integration) program modified a YF-16A (75-0750) with an advanced digital flight-control system and ventral canards. The airplane could perform tasks that had previously thought to be impossible, such as changing the angle or direction of the aircraft without changing its actual flight path. (NASA Dryden)

The AFTI YF-16A during a test flight on 6 March 1983. Along with the aerodynamic advancements such as the intake-mounted canards, the aircraft went on to test voice-controlled interaction and helmet-directed FLIR sensors. The AFTI YF-16A finished its career by flight-testing all-electric flight-control actuators for the Lockheed Martin F-35 Joint Strike Fighter (JSF). (NASA Dryden)

The first F-16XL was converted from the fifth YF-16A (75-0749) and flew for the first time on 3 July 1982. The second F-16XL was originally the third FSD F-16A (75-0747) modified with a two-seat F-16B cockpit. (AFFTC History Office Collection)

The second F-16XL (75-0747) wore a Ferris deceptive paint scheme for a while. This is the bottom – note the false canopy (with helmets!) and refueling receptacle outline. The aircraft is carrying two AIM-9 and four AIM-120 missiles. (AFFTC History Office Collection)

At the end of the Air Force flight-test program, both F-16XLs were turned over to NASA for other flight research duties. The distinctive white, black, and yellow paint scheme applied to the single-seat aircraft (75-0749) was done while on loan to the NASA Langley Research Center. Afterward, the F-16XLs were stored at the NASA Dryden Flight Research Center for several years. In 2007, the first F-16XL (now called NASA 849) was brought out of storage and taxied again to prepare it for potential flight-test work. (NASA Dryden)

After the YF-17 test program ended, both Northrop YF-17s were transferred to the NASA Dryden Flight Research Center for follow-on flight-testing. While the second YF-17 (72-1570) was used for spares, the first prototype (72-1569) was used for a variety of flight tests. Although the airplane was at NASA for less than two months (May to July 1976), the agency wasted no time in adding a NASA band and center name to both vertical stabilizers. (NASA Dryden)

The official rollout ceremony for the YF-17 took place at Northrop's Hawthorne, California, facility on 4 April 1974. The first YF-17 (72-1569) was then disassembled and trucked to Edwards to begin flight-testing. The 61-minute maiden flight took place on 9 June with Northrop test pilot Hank Chouteau at the controls. Two days later, the YF-17 became the first American jet fighter to fly supersonic in level flight without the use of afterburners. Contrast the subdued silver and black paint scheme to the bright red, white, and blue used by the YF-16. (Northrop)

Both YF-17s take their turn receiving fuel from a KC-97L. The second prototype (72-1570), in the foreground, sports a two-tone gray paint scheme. The first YF-17 is now on display at the Western Museum of Flight in Torrance, California, and the second is located at the U.S. Naval Aviation Museum in Pensacola, Florida. (AFFTC History Office Collection)

Powered by two General Electric YJ101s, the YF-17 had outstanding performance in the vertical. The YF-17 was the first aircraft that announced it could go supersonic in vertical flight, although the F-15 and F-16 could also perform the feat. (Northrop)

Although the YF-17 was not selected by the U.S. Air Force, the design was used as the basis for the McDonnell Douglas F/A-18 Hornet which has had a long and successful career with the U.S. Navy. (AFFTC History Office Collection)

The second Northrop F-20 (82-0063/N3986B) during a test flight. The F-20 had an internal fuel capacity of 5,050 pounds, and this could be augmented with three 275-gallon drop tanks. Production F-20s would have had the option of using the newly designed 330-gallon tanks along with two 50-gallon tip tanks similar to those used on the F-5A/B. (Northrop photo via Bill Norton)

Although the F-20 prototypes were not equipped with inflight aerial-refueling equipment, Northrop conducted air-refueling suitability tests behind a Marine Corps KC-130R (BuNo 160018) tanker. The third F-20 (82-0064/N44671) is shown flying behind the tanker as a Royal Saudi Air Force RF-5E takes on fuel. The similarities between the F-5 and F-20 are obvious. (Northrop photo via Bill Norton)

The third F-20, now sporting a light gray nose, taxis into its parking position on the Northrop ramp as the Space Shuttle Challenger is towed to the NASA Dryden Flight Research Center after landing at Edwards on 13 October 1984. (Northrop Grumman)

The first F-20 (82-0062/N4416T) banks over Edwards during an early test flight. Originally painted in a very flashy and distinctive red and white scheme, this was later changed to a more military-looking overall gray. (Northrop Grumman)

USAF Prototype Jet Fighters

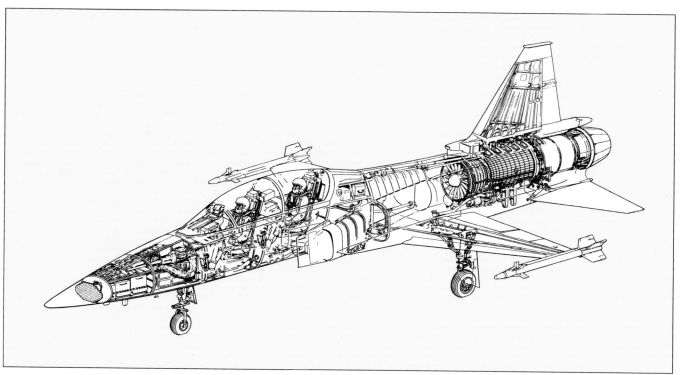

The F-20 Tigershark was originally designated as the F-5G, and the two-seat variant was known as the F-5H. The F-20 was powered by a single 16,000-lbf General Electric F404 turbofan engine and was fitted with the Westinghouse APG-67 radar. (Northrop via Ed Drumheller II)

The third F-20 parked on the Northrop ramp at Edwards. The aircraft appears to be carrying a Messerschmitt-Bolkow-Blohm modular dispenser system (MDS) that was derived from the MW-1 used on West German Tornados (Northrop via Bill Norton)

The three F-20s lined up on the ramp at Edwards. From front to back are Ship 2 (N3986B), Ship 1 (N4416T), and Ship 3 (N44671). Only the third airframe survived the program and is on diplay at the California Science Center in Los Angeles. (Northrop via Bill Norton)

Both Lockheed YF-22 prototypes in flight together. The two airframes were virtually identical except for markings, engines, and exhaust-nozzle assemblies. The red fixture on the first YF-22 is the spin recovery parachute container. (Lockheed Martin)

Late in its career, the second YF-22 had its Air Force serial number (87-0701) painted on its vertical stabilizer instead of the N-number (N22YX) that had been there for most of the flight-test program. (AFFTC History Office Collection)

This overhead front view of the first YF-22A (87-0700/N22YF) just prior to rollout shows the extreme angularity of the fuselage and intake surfaces. As rolled out, the YF-22 prototype did not have an engine. (Lockheed Martin photo by Eric Schulzinger)

A Pratt & Whitney YF119 during a ground run. This engine generated 35,000-lbf and had a two-dimensional nozzle with a thrust vectoring capability of ±20 degrees. The F119 was considered lower-risk than the competing General Electric YF120. (Pratt & Whitney)

The clean lines of the second YF-22 show up well in this view. Originally slated to be turned over to NASA, this airframe was damaged in a landing mishap and was eventually used as a pole model to measure the radar cross-section (RCS) of the F-22A. (Lockheed Martin)

The second YF-22 (87-0701/N22YX) in more-than-vertical flight. The second aircraft was powered by Pratt & Whitney YF119 engines, while the first aircraft used the competing General Electric YF120. The Pratt & Whitney engine won the competition. (Lockheed Martin)

In-flight refueling was used regularly throughout the test program to extend test missions and allow more test objectives to be achieved on each sortie. Here, the first YF-22 takes on fuel from a Boeing KC-135R (57-1469) tanker. (Lockheed Martin)

The first Lockheed YF-22 (87-0700/N22YF) and second Northrop YF-23 (87-0801/N232YF) fly formation for the first and only time on 18 December 1990. The difference in design concepts is clearly visible in the sharp angular surfaces of the YF-22 compared to the smooth, curved surfaces of the YF-23. This flight was the 16th and final flight of the second YF-23. (Air Force photo by SSgt. DJ Thompson)

The first YF-23 (87-0800/N231YF) heads to the runway at Edwards at the beginning of medium-speed taxi testing prior to first flight. Called PAV-1 (prototype air vehicle) by Northrop, the aircraft was painted overall dark gray and was powered by two Pratt & Whitney YF119 engines. (Northrop)

The cockpit of the first YF-23 shows a conventional layout of two displays, center-mounted control stick, and basic standby gauges. The majority of the instrumentation and the ejection seat were from a McDonnell Douglas F-15E, and the big-screen monitors proposed for production aircraft were not fitted. (Northrop via Bill Norton)

The second YF-23 shows its unique wing planform and large engine nacelles. PAV-2 made its first flight on 26 October 1990 and only flew 16 times for 21.6 hours before the flight-test program ended. The paint scheme was an overall two-tone light ghost gray, similar to early F-15s. (Northrop via Craig Kaston)

Like the YF-22, the YF-23s made use of aerial refueling to extend their test missions. This is the first YF-23A during its initial inflight refueling on 14 September 1990. The longest flight of the YF-23 program was 3.3 hours during flight number 13 on 23 October, flown by Bill Lowe. Note the Black Widow emblem. (Northrop)

The first YF-23 made its maiden flight at Edwards on 27 August 1990 with Northrop test pilot Paul Metz at the controls. Metz would later move to Lockheed Martin and make the first flight of the production F-22A. During the test program, PAV-1 made a total of 34 flights for 44.3 flight hours, including the final 6 flights that were made during a surge demonstration on 30 November. (Northrop)

The second YF-23 was powered by two General Electric YF120 engines and was used primarily for performance and maneuverability testing. It demonstrated a supercruise capability of Mach 1.6 on 29 November 1990. PAV-2 is on loan from NASA to the Western Museum of Flight in Torrance, California, but is currently stored at Northrop Grumman's facility in Hawthorne. (Northrop)

After spending nearly three years in storage at Edwards, both YF-23s were transferred to the NASA Dryden Flight Research Center on 1 December 1993. NASA funding for a planned structural test program on composite airframes never materialized. PAV-1 was returned to the Air Force and eventually ended up in the National Museum of the United States Air Force. (NASA photo by Jim Ross)

In the days before computers took over all of the computational fluid dynamics (CFD), tests were often performed in water tunnels with dyes injected at various points to predict airflow across the surfaces. In late 1991, NASA Dryden performed water-tunnel tests on models of the YF-22 and YF-23. Note the turbulence around the front of the engine nacelles on top of the fuselage. (NASA Dryden)

USAF Prototype Jet Fighters

Both YF-23 prototypes, flown by Paul Metz in PAV-1 and Jim Sandberg in PAV-2, fly over the Mojave Desert. *The different paint schemes on the two prototypes show up well in this view. The YF-23s flew a combined total of 50 flights for 65.9 flight hours.* (Northrop)

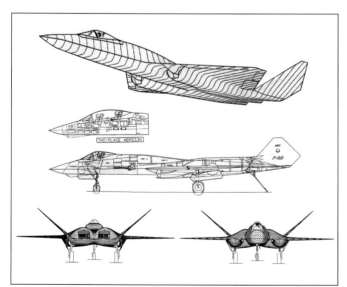

Unlike its Lockheed competitor, the F-23A EMD (engineering and manufacturing development) airplane would have had only relatively minor changes such as a slimmer aft fuselage profile and the addition of inlet shock cones. A two-seat variant was also proposed. (Northrop via Mike Hirschberg)

Artist concept of the two-seat F/B-23 Rapid Theater Attack proposal that was a response to Lockheed's F/B-22 interim attack bomber. The first glimpse of the F/B-23 came when a company model showed up for auction in February 2005, although it took Northrop more than six additional months to admit it. (Peter A. Barnett, Northrop Grumman)

The Boeing X-32A made its maiden flight from Palmdale to Edwards on 18 September 2000 with Boeing test pilot Fred Knox at the controls. Aerial refueling tests began in December using an Air Force KC-10 tanker. Both of the Boeing prototypes used the probe-and-drogue method of aerial refueling usually associated with Navy aircraft. Apparently, none of the X-32 or X-35 aircraft were assigned official serial numbers, and the Boeing aircraft also do not seem to have internal Boeing build numbers. (U.S. Air Force)

USAF Prototype Jet Fighters

One of the few angles from which the X-32A doesn't appear ungainly. The first supersonic flight of the X-32A was on 21 December 2000 when Lt. Col Edwards Cabrera took the aircraft to Mach 1.0 and 30,000 feet altitude. (U.S. Air Force)

The first X-32A prototype under construction at the Boeing Phantom Works facility in Palmdale. The nose inlet has not yet been fitted, but the rest of the airplane is relatively complete. The overall composite structure shows up well in this view. (Boeing)

The Boeing X-32B began its flight-test program with a flight from Palmdale to Edwards on 29 March 2001. Early in-flight high-altitude transitions began the following month. In May, the X-32B was flown from Edwards to NAS Patuxent River, Maryland, to conduct vertical landing tests. Due to the weight of the aircraft and the limited thrust from the left system, the X-32B could only conduct these tests at sea level and after numerous parts were removed to make the aircraft lighter. (U.S. Navy)

The X-32A performs a night engine run on the test stand at Edwards. The Pratt & Whitney F119-PW-614C engine produced approximately 35,000 lbf. (U.S. Air Force)

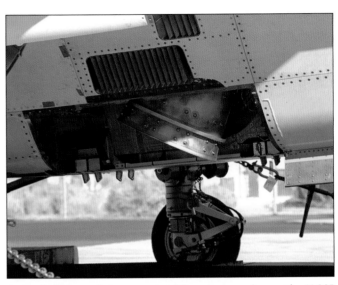

A good closeup of the vectoring lift-system nozzles on the X-32B STOVL demonstrator. During conventional flight, doors would be closed to cover the nozzles. (U.S. Navy)

The X-32B made its maiden flight on 29 March 2001 with Boeing test pilot Phil O'Donoughe at the controls of a 50-minute conventional flight from Palmdale to Edwards. Note the open doors for the vertical lift nozzles and the shortened wingspan of the X-32B. (U.S. Navy)

The X-32B performs hover testing at NAS Patuxent River. In order to complete these tests, a number of items had to be removed from the aircraft, including the inlet cowl, landing gear doors, and refueling probe. (U.S. Navy)

A view of the Boeing X-32A from a KC-10 boom operator's position. The X-32A was used to demonstrate the handling qualities of the Navy's aircraft carrier (CV) variant as well as the conventional-take-off-and-landing (CTOL) variant. (U.S. Air Force)

With its leading-edge slats and landing gear deployed, the X-32A comes in to land at Edwards. Commander Phillip "Rowdy" Yates and Fred Knox demonstrated carrier landings to a simulated carrier deck outlined on a runway at Edwards. (U.S. Air Force)

The final flight of the X-32A occurred on 3 February 2001 when the aircraft was ferried to Palmdale for storage. After four years of sitting outdoors in the desert sun, the aircraft was delivered to the National Museum of the United States Air Force in 2005. (Dennis R. Jenkins)

Even before the first prototype had flown, Boeing had changed the design of its production aircraft to a much more conventional layout as shown in this full-scale mockup. The risk associated with this change is one reason Lockheed Martin won the contract. (Boeing)

The Lockheed Martin X-35A (internal number 301) performs an in-flight refueling test from an NKC-135A (55-3135). The X-35A test program lasted just under one month before its conversion to the X-32B STOVL demonstrator. This aircraft is now in the collection of the National Air and Space Museum and is displayed at the Udvar-Hazy Center near Dulles International Airport in Washington, D.C. (U.S. Air Force)

The X-35C (internal number 300) made its first flight on 16 December 2000 from Palmdale to Edwards and was ferried to NAS Patuxent River in February 2001 to conduct aircraft-carrier suitability testing. (Lockheed Martin)

The X-35A was converted into the STOVL X-32B and began hover testing on 22 February 2001. On 23 July, RAF Squadron Leader Justin Paines performed a short takeoff, a supersonic dash, and vertical landing during two flights at Edwards. (Lockheed Martin)

Unlike the competing Boeing X-32, the X-35A was relatively sleek looking from any angle, as can been seen in this KC-135 boom operator's view. The X-35A made its first supersonic flight less than a month after its maiden flight. (U.S. Air Force)

During vertical landing testing at Edwards, the X-35B (301) used a two-seat TAV-8B Harrier as a chase plane. Note the JSF program and Skunk Works logos on the Harrier's vertical stabilizer. (Lockheed Martin photo by Tom Reynolds)

Nearly 50 years of technological development is shown in this Skunk Works family portrait at Palmdale. In front is the X-35A and (clockwise) are a U-2R, SR-71A, and F-117A. The original U-2, from which the U-2R was developed, was first flown in 1955, the SR-71 in 1964, the F-117A in 1981, and the X-35A in 2000. (Lockheed Martin photo by Denny Lombard)

The End